Cinderella

or The Sweet Little Maid And The Magic Shoes
or Love Is A Game That We Need Not Lose

A Victorian Pantomime

Alan Brown

Samuel French – London
New York – Sydney – Toronto – Hollywood

© 1986 BY ALAN BROWN

1. *This play is fully protected under the Copyright Laws of the British Commonwealth of Nations, the United States of America and all countries of the Berne and Universal Copyright Conventions.*

2. *All rights, including Stage, Motion Picture, Radio, Television, Public Reading and Translation into Foreign Languages, are strictly reserved.*

3. **No part of this publication may lawfully be reproduced in ANY form or by any means—photocopying, typescript, recording (including video-recording), manuscript, electronic, mechanical, or otherwise—or be transmitted or stored in a retrieval system, without prior permission.**

4. Rights of Performance by Amateurs are controlled by SAMUEL FRENCH LTD, 52 FITZROY STREET, LONDON W1P 6JR, and they, or their authorized agents, issue licences to amateurs to give performances of this play on payment of a fee. **It is an infringement of the Copyright to give any performance or public reading of the play before the fee has been paid and the licence issued.**

5. Licences are issued subject to the understanding that it shall be made clear in all advertising matter that the audience will witness an amateur performance; that the names of the authors of the plays shall be included on all announcements and on all programmes; and that the integrity of the author's work will be preserved.

   The Royalty Fee indicated below is subject to contract and subject to variation at the sole discretion of Samuel French Ltd.

   Basic fee for each and every
   performance by amateurs   Code M
   in the British Isles

   In Theatres or Halls seating Six Hundred or more the fee will be subject to negotiation.

   In Territories Overseas the fee quoted above may not apply. A fee will be quoted on application to our local authorized agent, or if there is no such agent, on application to Samuel French Ltd, London.

6. The Professional Rights in this play are controlled by INTERNATIONAL COPYRIGHT BUREAU LTD, Suite 8, 26 Charing Cross Road, London WC2 0DG.

The publication of this play does not imply that it is necessarily available for performance by amateurs or professionals, either in the British Isles or Overseas. Amateurs and professionals considering a production are strongly advised in their own interests to apply to the appropriate agents for consent before starting rehearsals or booking a theatre or hall.

ISBN 0 573 06475 X

CHARACTERS

Cinderella
Snowdrop ⎫
Tulip ⎭ her ugly sisters
Baron Hardup, her father
Polly Perkins, his niece
Buttons, his servant

Prince Charming
Dandini, the Prince's valet
Queen Mariana, the Prince's mother
Princess Andromeda, the Prince's cousin
Major-Domo

Wormwood ⎫
Scrubbs ⎭ the broker's men

Fairy Flora, Cinderella's fairy godmother
Aconite, a wicked fairy
Snow Queen
Fairies

Huntsmen, Villagers, Guests at the Ball, etc.

In the Harlequinade:

Harlequin
Columbine (Polly Perkins)
Pierrot (Buttons)
Pantaloon (Baron)
Clown (Scrubbs)
Butcher (Wormwood)
Watchman (Major-Domo)
Lady

SYNOPSIS OF SCENES

PART I
SCENE 1 A fairy glen
SCENE 2 The forest in winter
SCENE 3 The forest in summer
SCENE 4 The road to Hardup Hall
SCENE 5 The kitchen in Hardup Hall
SCENE 6 The ugly sisters' boudoir
SCENE 7 The kitchen in Hardup Hall

PART II
SCENE 8 A road outside the royal palace
SCENE 9 The royal ballroom
SCENE 9a Harlequinade
SCENE 10 A room in Hardup Hall
SCENE 11 The royal palace (Cinderella's wedding)

MUSICAL NUMBERS

The song titles which are contained in this list are non-copyright and, where possible, the publishers of the music are given in brackets after the title.

Alan Brown has produced a separate list of song suggestions for use with this pantomime which is available free of charge upon application to Samuel French Ltd. However, please remember that a licence issued by Samuel French Ltd to perform this pantomime does NOT include permission to use copyright songs and music. Please read the notice supplied by the Performing Right Society which follows on page vii.

PART I

Overture		Orchestra
No. 1	**Hail to Phoebus**	Fairy Flora
No. 2		Dandini and Chorus
No. 3		Prince Charming and Cinderella
No. 4		Tulip and Snowdrop
No. 5	**Beer, Beer, Glorious Beer** (Francis, Day & Hunter)	Baron
No. 6		Buttons
No. 7	**There's A Hole In My Bucket**	Wormwood and Scrubbs
No. 8	**Father's A Drunkard And Mother Is Dead**	Cinderella, Baron and Trio
No. 9	**Let Me Kiss Her For Her Mother**	Fairy Flora and Chorus
No. 10		Tulip, Snowdrop, Wormwood and Scrubs
No. 11		Buttons and Cinders
No. 12	**Fairy Daughter by Heaven Blessed**	Flora, Aconite and Company

PART II

No. 13	**Our Motor's Broken Down** (to the tune of John Brown's Body)	Baron, Tulip and Snowdrop
No. 14		Prince Charming
No. 15		Prince Charming and Cinderella

No. 16	**After The Ball** (Francis, Day & Hunter)	Baron, Andromeda, Polly and Company
No. 17		Tulip and Snowdrop
No. 18		Buttons and Cinderella
No. 19		Queen, Baron, Andromeda, Buttons, Dandini and Polly
Walk Down Song 2 (reprise)		Prince Charming and Cinderella
Finale	**After the Ball** (reprise)	Company

If you have any difficulty obtaining sheet music, FRANCIS MUSIC SUPPLY, 12 Gerrard Street, London W1, are most helpful.

The following statement concerning the use of music is printed here on behalf of the Performing Right Society Ltd, by whom it was supplied

The permission of the owner of the performing right in copyright music must be obtained before any public performance may be given, whether in conjunction with a play or sketch or otherwise, and this permission is just as necessary for amateur performances as for professional. The majority of copyright musical works (other than oratorios, musical plays and similar dramatico-musical works) are controlled in the British Commonwealth by the PERFORMING RIGHT SOCIETY LTD, 29–33 BERNERS STREET, LONDON W1P 4AA.

The Society's practice is to issue licences authorizing the use of its repertoire to the proprietors of premises at which music is publicly performed, or, alternatively, to the organizers of musical entertainments, but the Society does not require payment of fees by performers as such. Producers or promoters of plays, sketches, etc., at which music is to be performed, during or after the play or sketch, should ascertain whether the premises at which their performances are to be given are covered by a licence issued by the Society, and if they are not, should make application to the Society for particulars as to the fee payable.

PRODUCTION NOTE

To set the period it is suggested that during the arrival of the audience an advertisement cloth is displayed bearing 1890's period advertisements by local shops and firms still in existence today. Immediately prior to the rise of the Curtain the advertisement cloth is raised, and a Victorian stage manager comes from behind the Curtain with a lighted taper and ignites the (imitation) footlights.

To
David Drummond
—for so generously sharing his "Pleasures of Past Times"

PART I*

Scene 1

A fairy glen (gauze frontcloth). Night

The moon is in evidence

Fairy Flora enters R

Flora Come forth, my fairy elves,
 And trip a dainty measure,
 While yet the darkness mantles us,
 And gives us time for pleasure.

Fairies—spirits of the flowers—enter, variously arrayed

 Sweet Spirits of the Flowers,
 Your faithful homage tender,
 And I will tell a service which
 To mortal you may render.
Fairies Tell us, dear Queen, what we may do
 To please ourselves and honour you.
Flora There is a little maid
 Who dwells in yonder house;
 I need your fairy aid
 Her welfare to espouse.
 She is so good and sweet,
 Tho' garbed in rough prunella,
 Her virtues are complete,
 Her name is Cinderella.
Fairies Her name is Cinderella!
 Then tell her, Fairy, tell her
 Our loving services we press
 On her to give her happiness.
Flora To aid her I will take an early chance,
 And now, my elves, a ring of fay we'll dance.

Aconite enters

Aconite Hold!!!
Flora Who is it dares to interrupt our rite?
Fairies 'Tis Aconite!!
Flora Wolfsbane! A rebel 'gainst our power!

---

*N.B. Paragraph 3 on page ii of this Acting Edition regarding photocopying and video-recording should be carefully read.

Aconite The same. The king of every noisome flower!
So stay thy revels!
Take one word of warning,
I reign supreme
From midnight to the morning.
This mortal child who claims your aid
I hate, because she's good;
When *midnight* strikes I'm much afraid
That will be understood!
If Cinderella shall at any time
Remain abroad beyond the midnight chime,
Your fairy powers avail not, so beware,
For Aconite his vengeance shall prepare!
Flora Begone!
Fairies Begone!!
Aconite At the midnight hour,
When each noisome flower
Exhales its poison in the chill night air;
When grisly hosts
Of shrouded ghosts
In phantom revels join—beware!

The Lights begin to change

Flora I fear you not. I treat your threats with scorn.
Your power is fled, behold the breaking dawn!

Aconite flees

Musical background

Song No. 1 Hail to Phoebus

(*Chanting*) Hail to Phoebus, who from slumber
Wakes to paint the roseate dawn,
Fading stars whom none can number
By the magic of his scorn.
Hail to Phoebus and his pageant
As they sweep across the skies,
Heralded by feathered songsters,
Bidding life from sleep to rise.
Hail the light!
Fairies Hail the light!

Wind and snow effect. The Fairies cower and shiver DR, *covering their heads*

The Snow Queen is revealed in icy splendour behind the gauze

The Lights fade up on:

Scene 2

The forest in winter (three-quarter stage with gauze backcloth upstage)

Part I, Scene 2

Snow lighting effect and the low sound of icy wind

Fairies The icy breath of winter
Still covers all the land;
It grips the trees and flowers
As in an iron band.
The merry birds are silent,
All nature's still and dumb,
And shivering toilers murmur
"Will springtime never come?"

The gauze frontcloth from Scene 1 is raised

Flora Still here, Snow Queen? Why do you linger? Do not the cries of the starving poor melt your cold heart, and inspire you with pity for their sufferings?

Snow Queen Pity? Why should I pity them? Is there a single one that regards me in any other light than that of an enemy? Fools! If Nature were always clad in leafy raiment, where would be the gladness of the Spring?—the golden glory of the Autumn? Of all the seasons mine alone is unwelcome to mankind.

Flora Because you have stayed too long. Dame Nature, expectant, waits for Spring, but though a generous hostess, she can entertain but one guest at a time. Surely you will not be so churlish as to keep Spring waiting at her door?

Snow Queen I will depart at no-one's bidding. Until I hear a human voice extolling my beauty I shall remain.

The Snow Queen exits

Flora Be mine the task to find some mortal whose gentle words shall melt her heart of ice, and bring sweet sunshine to the earth once more!

Hunting horns, off, and sounds of the chase

But hark! The Royal Hunt!
The youthful Prince, from foreign lands returned,
Pursues the chase along the diamond forest.
His parents' will (besides his subjects' good)
Bids him to choose for partner a Princess—
But I have fixed on her whom he must wed,
The mortal daughter whom your Queen befriends.

The horns are heard again, nearer

Fly swift, invisible to earthly eyes,
Withdraw the Prince from all—then guide him here.

The Fairies exit

Where to his sight her image shall be shown
Who shall tomorrow share his heart and throne.

Flora exits

The orchestra plays the "Hunting Chorus"

Dandini and the Huntsmen enter. Dandini is elegantly dressed and sports a monocle

Dandini (*yawning*) This early rising is a bally awful fag. I never see the sense of thirty or forty Johnnies getting up in the middle of the night to run after one poor, unfortunate pig.
Huntsman Probably the pig would agree with you, Dandini.
Dandini Wrong, my boy! Pig always *dis*agrees with me! (*He pats his stomach*)

All laugh

What has become of the Prince?
Huntsman I saw him a few minutes ago talking to one of the keepers.
Dandini His predilection for that class of person is astounding.

Screams, off

Huntsman What's that?
Dandini Sounds like a lovely woman in distress. Gentlemen, leave this to me.

Polly Perkins and village maidens run on, screaming "Save us! Save us!"

What's the matter? (*He has one arm round Polly, and one round another girl*)
Polly A horrid wild boar!
Huntsman Where?
All Girls There!!
Polly Oh! He's gone now!
Dandini Don't be afraid, gals. I will protect you. (*He chucks Polly under her chin*)
Polly Oh? Who might you be?
Dandini Dandini!
All Girls Who?
Dandini The Prince's personal valet, don't yer know. The Right Honourable Algernon, Dando, Orlando, Davy, Dandini!
Girl Dan Leno?

They all crowd round him

Dandini Dandini! I'm frightfully well known at the Palace of course, but no matter where Dame Fortune deigns to direct me, there's one place you'll always find Dandini.
All Girls Where's that?
Dandini I'll tell you ... (*He sings*)

Song No. 2

The Stage Manager enters with the words on an easel

The cast and audience sing the final chorus together

Everyone exits

Part I, Scene 2

A hunting horn is heard, off. Fairy music

The Fairies enter, drawing on the Prince. The Fairies exit

Prince Throughout my pilgrimage of foreign lands I never saw a place of more romantic beauty. If ever there was a charmed spot of fairy haunt this is the one. The air is perfume, icicles sparkle with the rainbow's hue from every tree, and, as my willing steps advanced, a strain of melody sighed on my ear and drew me on to follow . . . (*Calling*) Dandini! Are you near?

The Prince blows the horn. More Fairy music

This place doth seem
The proper sort of place for Love's young dream.
Banish such thoughts! Such love just cannot be!
Where to find *true* love? That is the mystery.

Song No. 3

The Prince sings

As he does so, Fairy Flora appears upstage, close to the backcloth

At an appropriate point in the song Fairy Flora raises her wand

Cinderella appears behind the gauze backcloth with a basket of daisies (as in the Prince's dream) and sings the chorus

The Prince turns and sees Cinderella singing. Finally, he sings with her

(*Speaking*) What a beautiful vision! (*He kneels*) Mortal or Goddess, receive my homage! Let me for ever gaze upon those celestial features, and with my daring hand remove the mist!

He advances towards the gauze. Fairy Flora appears visibly before him. The music continues

Flora Hold!
Prince What art thou?
Flora One that will prove thy friend if thou deserve it.
For her whom thou would'st now approach, go and seek her
Where thou mayst do so openly and free!
If thou preferest virtue unto wealth
Goodness and modesty to heartless grandeur,
Thou mayst e'en this day find her; till then, lose her!
(*She raises her wand*)

Cinderella disappears

But bear her features living in thy heart!

Horn, off, approaching

Thy friends now seek thee and approach this spot;

Their eyes must not behold us. Prince, farewell!
As thus I touch thee with my rod of might,
Let thine eyes close awhile upon the light!
Let all that's passed to thy remembrance seem
On thy awakening as thy fancy's dream!

She touches the Prince with her wand. He reclines to sleep

Fairy Flora exits

Dandini enters

Dandini Your Highness! Your Highness! I say, are you feeling a bit dicky?
Prince (*waking*) Ha! Dandini! Friend! Was it all then but a dream?
Dandini Your Highness?
Prince Did you see anyone leave this place?
Dandini None, your Highness.
Prince (*aside*) Then farewell happiness!
Dandini Perk up, your Highness! You must have just nodded off, don't yer know. That's what comes of gettin' up with the bally lark. Sorry if I disturbed your repose.
Prince That repose may prove my curse forever! Where's the rest of the hunt?
Dandini I think I hear them coming.

Sound of a fast galloping horse followed by loud crash, neighs and yells

Snowdrop (*off*) Clumsy Cow! Now look what you've done!
Tulip (*off*) Who're you calling a cow? You freckle-faced faggot!
Dandini Oh, no!
Snowdrop (*off*) If I had a face like yours I'd put it against a wall and throw a brick at it!
Tulip (*off*) If I had a face like yours I'd put it against a brick and throw a wall at it!
Prince Who is it?
Snowdrop (*off*) Clodpole!
Tulip (*off*) Bacon Bonce!
Prince *What* is it?
Dandini You mean Animal or Vegetable?
Snowdrop (*off*) Ooooooooo!
Dandini Animal—definitely! It's the Baron Hardup's two ugly daughters—fighting as usual.
Snowdrop (*off*) Ooooooooh look! It *is*—isn't it?
Tulip (*off*) Ooooooooh, it *isn't*—is it?
Dandini And I fear they've spotted us, your Highness.
Prince "Us"? Yes "us"! You've given me an idea. I'll wager they have no idea which of us is which!
Dandini Your Highness flatters me!
Prince We'll quickly see. Pretend to be me. (*He exchanges their hats*)
Dandini (*dismayed*) Eh?

Mock hunting music: (few bars from Wagner's "Ride of the Valkyries")

Part I, Scene 2

The ugly sisters, dressed in bizarre hunting attire, swoop on and curtsy very low—less of a curtsy than a collapse

Snowdrop Your Princeship!
Tulip Your Flagship!

The Prince nudges Dandini

Dandini Er ... Whom are you addressing ... er ... ladies?
Snowdrop Why, your High and Mightyness——
Tulip The Prince!
Snowdrop We hope!
Dandini Ah! I see you recognize royal blood when you meet it. Arise!
Snowdrop Oh, bless your little cotton socks, I should know you anywhere from Papa's prescription. Permit us, me lud, to traduce ourselves. I am Snowdrop.
Tulip And I'm Tulip, your Holiness.
Prince The Baron Hardup's very unusual daughters, don't yer know.
Snowdrop How sweet of you to dismember us!
Tulip Who, may I ask, is the other nob?
Dandini Er ... Dandini—my valet.
Prince At your service, ladies. (*He bows*)
Snowdrop Oh, is that all! (*She pushes the Prince to one side and crosses to the other side of Dandini*) I thought he looked a bit common.
Dandini I trust you ladies are enjoying the hunt.
Snowdrop Oh superslobidobs! (*She curtsies*)
Tulip Likewise! (*She curtsies*)
Dandini Well if you'll excuse me, ladies, I must return to the Palace. (*He crosses to exit*)
Snowdrop Of course, of course, your Worship. Do come and call on us some time and inscribe in a cup of tea.
Dandini I shall see you tonight at the Ball?
Tulip Oooh, yes!
Snowdrop We'll be there!
Dandini (*aside*) I was afraid of that! (*Aloud*) Ladies!
Snowdrop (*curtsying*) Your Princeship!
Tulip (*likewise*) Your Flagship!

Dandini bows, raises his eyes to heaven at the Prince, and exits

Prince (*bowing*) Ladies!
Snowdrop (*grandly*) Were you speaking to us?
Prince Why yes!
Snowdrop Well don't let it occur again!

The Prince exits

Tulip Did you see him? Did you see him smile at me?
Snowdrop Who?
Tulip The Prince of course. He smiled at me.
Snowdrop Don't be ... Why should he smile at *you*?
Tulip He was excited.

Snowdrop Don't be ridiculous. You're only exciting to another idiot.
Tulip Now what should I do to make the Prince marry me?
Snowdrop Chloroform him! Anyway, it was me he was smiling at—not you!
Tulip It was me! It was me!
Snowdrop Some chance! Why that phiz would frighten a fuzzy-wuzzy!
Tulip Lies and filth!
Snowdrop Oh? What about young Josh then?
Tulip Oh, you're not going to bring Josh up again!
Snowdrop Go on, tell them what happened.
Tulip That's not fair!

Song No. 4

Tulip and Snowdrop sing

> *At the end of the verse the Stage Manager enters with the words of the chorus on an easel*

Snowdrop invites the audience to join in and conducts them as Tulip sings. Then Tulip and Snowdrop sing the next verse with everyone singing the final chorus

> *Everyone exits at the end of the song*

Music

> *Cinderella enters, hunting for firewood*

Cinderella What shall I do? What shall I do? Someone has been before me and gathered all the sticks, and if I return home without any my stepsisters will beat me. I try so hard to please them but it is all in vain. (*She continues to look for wood*)

Aconite appears

Cinderella shivers and pulls her shawl closer round herself

Aconite (*aside*) Cinderella!
See how she shrinks from me as though in fear!
Instinct seems to warn her that I am here.
I hate the drudge, and while she hither dwells
I'll warp her mind with my most loathsome spells!

Flora enters

Flora Stay your hand!
Aconite So you've come to interfere!
Flora To shield her from danger I'm always near.
Thy presence casts a blight on every flower.
Dogsbane, begone!
Aconite Bah! Come the midnight hour
You both shall feel the venom of my power!

Aconite exits

Part I, Scene 3

Fairy Flora disguises herself as an old woman

Cinderella Even Papa has ceased to take any notice of me now. I seem to be all alone in the world. All alone. If only some good fairy would come along and help me. But they say there's no such thing as fairies. (*She has succeeded in adding to her bundle of sticks*)

Flora (*disguised*) Fair Cinderella, be so good,
And let me have some sticks of wood!
My blood is chilled, my bones are old,
My house is damp, and I am cold!

Cinderella Poor old dame! Take these. (*She gives Flora her bundle of sticks*) Please! I can easily find more.

Flora Ah, child, you are very kind.

Cinderella How did you know my name?

Flora Not all of Nature's ways are known to the young.

Cinderella You're not a witch, are you?

Flora Some call me that, but have no fear, I wish you naught but good.

Cinderella Why do they call you a witch?

Flora Because I am old and ugly, and have neither kith nor kin. Some blame me because the Winter has been so long.

Cinderella Poor old soul! May I come and see you sometimes?

Flora Bless your kind heart.

Cinderella I am poor and almost friendless too. My only happy days are spent here in the forest.

Flora Ay, in the warmth and glow of Summer.

Cinderella No, at all seasons!

The Lights come up slowly behind the gauze to reveal the Snow Queen standing behind Cinderella. Low hiss of cymbals from the orchestra

To me the forest is never more beautiful than now, when the branches of the trees are laden with snow, and every drop of water becomes a sparkling diamond!

Soft music. The Lights come up slowly on the backcloth revealing:

Scene 3

The forest in summer (fullstage)

During the following the Snow Queen raises her arms in satisfied triumph, and with a gesture relinquishes her hold over the elements, and exits

Flora Ah child! You have the warm and generous heart that sees beauty in all that surround it. Look! Your words have melted even the icy heart of the Snow Queen, who relinquished her iron grasp of the land, and speeds away to the far North. Hark how the birds carol forth their welcome to Spring. All Nature rejoices that the long dreary Winter is past. Take courage, child. As the shades of Winter depart from the Earth so shall the clouds pass away from your young life, and happiness reign supreme!

Flora exits. The Spirits of the Flowers, above the gauze, unfold gently, and begin to dance joyously

Cinderella Oh how beautiful! How lovely! Why the kind old woman has gone, and I do not even know where to find her again. How sorry I am. Never mind. I cannot be sad any more today, for the sunshine has gladdened my heart!

The winter gauze rises. Humming chorus. Cinderella dances a "Spring ballet" with the Spirits of the Flowers. Music: "Pas de Deux" (Andante maestoso), "Intrada" for "Sugar Plum Fairy and Cavalier" from the last Act of The Nutcracker Suite *by Tchaikovsky*

Scene 4

The road to Hardup Hall (frontcloth)

The Baron enters, drunk, carrying a letter, and mopping his eyes with a large spotted handkerchief

Baron Oh dear, oh dear, oh dear, oh dear . . . ! Oh dear, oh dear, oh dear, oh dear! Ruined! Ruined!!! Why did I ever invest my money in that Opera House? Gone! Every penny! I shall be sold up! Sold up! Wait till my daughters find out! They'll skin me! They'll blame it all on the drink. If you should see my daughters about anywhere, take 'em away and lose 'em! Whenever I see those two girls of mine I want to shriek for the steward. I say I want to shriek for the steward! I could just do with a pint now! Ah, drink . . . ! I'm going to tell you something now. I'm going to confide in you. If there's any of you delicate I wouldn't advise you to stay. You can ask for your money back. I say you can *ask* for your money back. You won't get it but you can *ask*!

Song No. 5 Beer, Beer, Glorious Beer
by S. Leggett and W. Godwin

(*Singing*) Now I won't sing of sherbert and water,
For sherbert with beer will not rhyme;
When you're broke you can't afford champagne,
It's a bit more than two "D" a time;
So I'll sing you a song of a gargle,
A gargle that I love so dear,
I allude to that grand institution,
That beautiful tonic called beer, beer, beer.

Beer, beer, glorious beer!
Fill yourselves right up to here!
Drink a good deal of it, make a good meal of it,
Stick to your old-fashioned beer!
Don't be afraid of it, drink till you're made of it,

Part I, Scene 4

> Now all together a cheer!
> Up with the sale of it, down with a pale of it,
> Glorious, glorious, beer!!

(*Patter*) Oh dear, no, I mean let's think about it. Sherioushly! Let's take the evils of drink. I may tell you that I'm a man who for years has set his face against drink. Look at that lip! A pot rester! Doctors are always telling us that drinking shortens your life. I don't believe it. I mean let's face it, you see a lot more old drunks than old doctors, don't you . . . ? I went to a temperance lecture once, and the lecturer took two live worms, and put one in a glass of water and it lived. He put the other one in a glass of gin and it died. He said: "There my friends, the one in the water lived, and the one in the gin died. Now what does that prove?" I said: "If you've got worms, drink gin!" (*He sings*)

> It's the daddy of all lubricators
> The best thing there is for your neck—
> Can be used as a gargle or lotion
> By persons of every sect,
> Now we know who the goddess of wine was,
> But was there a goddess of beer?
> If so let us drink to her health, boys,
> And wish that we'd just got her here, here, here!

The Stage Manager enters with the words of the chorus on an easel

The Baron sings with the audience

Baron } Beer, beer glorious beer! *etc.*
Audience

Baron (*speaking*) Fine thing! My beautiful daughters scooted with the ancestral barouche so now I've got to walk home! Ah, my little Cinders would never have left me like that. Which reminds me, I've got something else on my mind. (*He removes his hat and takes a kipper from it*) It's been there since last Good Friday. I intended it as a surprise for Cinders. Never mind, the next time Buttons complains about his victuals I'll give him this. (*He hangs the kipper on his ear*) By the way, where is that scallywag? Buttons!! Buttons!!

Buttons, the Baron's pageboy, enters and moves to the Baron's side

Buttons Here, Baron.
Baron Buttons!! Oh! There you are! Whatever kept you?
Buttons Baron, what is that fish doing on your ear?
Baron Eh?
Buttons (*louder*) What is that fish doing on your ear?
Baron Oh, that's my new herring aid! Now Buttons, you've got to help me!
Buttons Sir?
Baron Buttons, I'm ruined. I, your master, am ruined!! Ruined!!
Buttons Oh, don't say that, sir.

Baron I do say it! If I don't square things today, we shall all be thrown out tomorrow!
Buttons You'll never find another place like Hardup Hall, sir.
Baron You're right, my boy. I could never settle in.
Buttons Or settle up! Which reminds me, Baron, there's the matter of my back pay, sir.
Baron Back pay? Oh come now, don't let's quarrel about your back pay.
Buttons No, sir. There wouldn't be very much to quarrel about if we did. I haven't eaten properly for three days!
Baron Well then force yourself, my boy, force yourself! (*Crossing to exit*) I simply must live in a house that overlooks the woods, *and* overlooks the river...

The Baron exits

Buttons *And* overlooks the rent! Poor old Baron! But it's true what he says. He's so broke *he* can't even afford to spend Christmas. (*He sees the audience*) Oh, hello! Let me introduce myself. I'm Buttons. I work for the Baron. Things are really bad up at the Hall. Last week the landlord came round to tell the Baron he was going to raise the rent. "Thank the Lord," says the Baron, " 'cos I can't!" And if that wasn't enough there's his terrible stepdaughters Snowdrop and Tulip. Well, they're always so temperamental! Snowdrop's always in a temper, and Tulip's mental. Not like their little stepsister Cinderella! She's beautiful! Ahhhhh! Don't *you* think she's beautiful? Ahhhhh! I'll tell you a secret (*Confidentially*) I love Cinderella!
Audience Ahhhhhh!
Buttons She reminds me of my dear old mother!
Audience Ahhhhhh!
Buttons Oh, it's all right for you to make fun. But if my old dad were still alive *he*'d understand! (*He sings*)

Song No. 6

After the second chorus the Stage Manager enters with the words of the chorus on an easel

Buttons sings with the audience. Then the audience repeat the chorus while Buttons dances

(*Speaking*) So now you know! Tell you what! Why don't you and me be pals? 'Cos I'm going to need a few pals before this show's over, I can tell you! Here's what we do: every time I come on up here I'll shout out "Hello, kids!" and you shout back "Hello, Buttons!". Right? Come on, let's try it.

Buttons exits and returns

Hello, kids!
Audience (*muttering*) Hello, Buttons.
Buttons Oh, come on! You can do better than that. Mums and Dads too! As

Part I, Scene 4

loud as you can. Show your teeth, show your teeth . . . I said show them, lady, not pass them round! Ready?

Buttons exits and returns carrying a pair of brightly coloured boots

Hello, kids!
Audience Hello, Buttons!
Buttons Ah, that's better! Now here's another way you can help me. See these? They're the Baron's boots. I've just finished polishing them. Just look at that shine! Now I don't want anyone messing about with those boots, 'cos they take a lot of polishing. So I'll put them down here—and if anyone touches 'em you all shout out "Don't touch" really loud! Will you? Come on then, let's have a practice. Pretend I'm not me—pretend I'm Rudyard Kipling and I'm just mad about boots! Here we go! (*He approaches the boots*)
Audience Don't touch! *etc., etc.*
Buttons That's fine! Just fine!

Wormwood, a broker's man, enters and goes to C

Wormwood I say, I say, I say! (*He spots the boots, and doubles back to approach them*)
Audience Don't touch!
Wormwood (*whipping out a notebook and pencil*) Right then! (*Making a note*) One pair of boots—untouched!
Buttons Yes, sir? Can I assist you?
Wormwood Is this the way to Hardup Hall?

Scrubbs, the second broker's man, enters, wearing a bowler hat from which two small horns protrude, and carrying a wooden bucket with a hole. He spies the boots and approaches them

Audience Don't touch!

Song No. 7 There's A Hole In My Bucket

The following verses and patter should be played very slickly and with good pace, unaccompanied by music

Wormwood Yes?
Scrubbs (*singing*) There's a hole in my bucket
              Dear Wormwood, dear Wormwood,
              There's a hole in my bucket,
              Dear Wormwood—a hole!
Wormwood   Then mend it, dear Oscar,
              Dear Oscar, dear Oscar,
              Then mend it, dear Oscar,
              Dear Oscar—mend it!

Scrubbs crosses to exit, then turns and sings

Scrubbs   With what shall I mend it,
                    Dear Wormwood, dear Wormwood,
                    With what shall I mend it,
                    Dear Wormwood—with what?
Wormwood   With straw, dear Oscar,
                    Dear Oscar, dear Oscar,
                    With straw, dear Oscar,
                    Dear Oscar—with straw!

Scrubbs exits

(*Speaking*) As I was saying, is this the way to Hardup Hall?

Scrubbs returns with straw

Scrubbs (*singing*) The straw is too long,
                    Dear Wormwood, dear Wormwood,
                    The straw is too long,
                    Dear Wormwood—too long!
Buttons (*indicating Scrubbs' hat*) Pardon me, sir, but what sort of hat is dat?
Wormwood That's his "demon bowler".
(*Singing*)   Then cut it, dear Oscar,
                    Dear Oscar, dear Oscar,
                    Then cut it dear Oscar,
                    Dear Oscar—cut it!
Scrubbs   With what shall I cut it,
                    Dear Wormwood, dear Wormwood,
                    With what shall I cut it,
                    Dear Wormwood—with what?
Wormwood (*speaking*) I know you'd never believe this, but this lad is descended from a fine old pioneering family.
Buttons Oh, yes?
Wormwood Oh, yes. His father was known as Bicarbonate Brown.
Buttons Bicarbonate Brown!
Wormwood One of the early settlers.
(*Singing*)   With a knife, dear Oscar,
                    Dear Oscar, dear Oscar,
                    With a knife, dear Oscar,
                    Dear Oscar—a knife!

Scrubbs exits

(*Speaking to Buttons*) Now then, is this the way to Hardup Hall?
Buttons Who wants to know?
Wormwood (*producing a card*) Wormwood and Scrubbs—broker's men.
Buttons (*aghast*) Broker's men!!!

Scrubbs enters with a knife

Scrubbs (*singing*) The knife is too blunt,
                    Dear Wormwood, dear Wormwood,
                    The knife is too blunt,
                    Dear Wormwood—too blunt!

Part I, Scene 4

Buttons (*speaking*) Did you say Broker's Men?!
Wormwood That's right. I'm Wormwood, and this is Scrubbs. He's the brains of the organization. That'll give you some idea of the organization!
  (*Singing*)   Then sharpen it, dear Oscar,
           Dear Oscar, dear Oscar,
           Then sharpen it, dear Oscar,
           Dear Oscar—sharpen it!
Scrubbs   With what shall I sharpen it,
           Dear Wormwood, dear Wormwood,
           With what shall I sharpen it,
           Dear Wormwood—with what?
Wormwood (*speaking*) I'm afraid he's a little naïve.
Buttons Oh yes?
Wormwood Oh, yes. Until quite recently he thought that sex was what the coalman brings the coal in.
  (*Singing*)   With a stone, dear Oscar,
           Dear Oscar, dear Oscar,
           With a stone, dear Oscar,
           Dear Oscar—with a stone.

Scrubbs exits

Buttons Why do you want Hardup Hall?
Wormwood The Baron owes hire purchase money on all his furniture.
Buttons Ah, these are hard times.
Wormwood Very hard. Remember what the chicken said when she laid a square egg.
Buttons What did the chicken say when she laid a square egg?
Wormwood Ouch!!!

Scrubbs returns with a stone

Scrubbs (*singing*) The stone is too dry,
           Dear Wormwood, dear Wormwood,
           The stone is too dry,
           Dear Wormwood—too dry!
Wormwood Then wet it, dear Oscar,
           Dear Oscar, dear Oscar,
           Then wet it, dear Oscar,
           Dear Oscar—wet it!
Scrubbs   With what shall I wet it,
           Dear Wormwood, dear Wormwood,
           With what shall I wet it,
           Dear Wormwood—with what?
Buttons (*speaking*) Why do you call him Oscar?
Wormwood Oh, that's not his real name.
Buttons Oh? What is his real name?
Wormwood Tell him!
Scrubbs Abklmunch—dj!
Buttons I beg your pardon??
Scrubbs Abklmunch—dj!

Buttons Abkl—no I can't! Say it again!
Wormwood (*producing a card*) Here! Abklmuch—dj!
Buttons (*reading from the card*) "Abklmunch ...
Wormwood —dj!
Buttons —dj!
Wormwood Abklmunch—dj!
Buttons How'd he get a name like that?
Wormwood His father was an optician!

Scrubbs nudges him with the stone

(*Singing*)   With water, dear Oscar,
              Dear Oscar, dear Oscar,
              With water, dear Oscar,
              Dear Oscar—with water.

Scrubbs crosses to the exit

(*Speaking*) So which is the way to Hardup Hall?
Buttons You're really going to take all the Baron's furniture?
Wormwood When we've finished with him he won't even have a roof to his mouth.
Buttons (*pointing the wrong way*) Straight back the way you come—second on the left!

Scrubbs appears and sings

Scrubbs   In what shall I get it,
               Dear Wormwood, dear Wormwood,
               In what shall I get it,
               Dear Wormwood—in what?
Wormwood (*crossing to him*)
               In a bucket, dear Oscar,
               Dear Oscar, dear Oscar,
               In a bucket, dear Oscar,
               Dear Oscar—in a bucket!

Scrubbs exits but returns immediately with the bucket

Scrubbs (*singing*) There's a hole in my bucket,
               Dear Wormwood, dear Wormwood,
               There's a hole in my bucket,
               Dear Wormwood, a——!!

But Wormwood has reversed the bucket over Scrubbs's head and marches him off

The orchestra finishes Scrubbs's last note for him as a final chord

Buttons shrugs and exits in the opposite direction

The frontcloth rises to reveal:

Scene 5

The kitchen in Hardup Hall (fullstage)

There is a very large fireplace in the UC *wall with a stool or small chair to one side, windows in the* UL *and* UR *walls, and entrances* DL *and* DR. *A large basket skip stands* RC, *a kitchen table* URC *covered with a large red chequered tablecloth, a chest* UL *and a cupboard large enough to take the required articles*

Tableau vivant: the Baron sits with his head and arms spread over the kitchen table. An empty rum bottle stands beside one hand. Polly and two villagers (a close harmony trio) stand DLC. *Cinderella sits on the chair beside the fireplace, peeling potatoes as she sings*

Song No. 8 Father's A Drunkard and Mother Is Dead
(Written by "Stella" and composed by Mrs E. A. Parkhurst)

Cinderella	Out of the gloomy wood gladly I'd roam—
	I have no Mother, no pleasant home,
	Nobody cares for me, no-one would cry
	Even if poor little Cinders should die;
	Barefoot and tired I'd wander all day
	Asking for work—But I'm too small they say.
	In this cruel house I must still lay my head—
	Father's a Drunkard and Mother is dead!
Cinderella and the Trio	Mother, oh! why did you leave me (her) alone?
	With no-one to love me (her), no friends and no home?
	Dark is the night and the storm rages wild,
	God pity Cinders, the Drunkard's lone child!
Baron	She was so happy until I drank rum,
	Then all her sorrow and trouble begun;
	Mother grew paler and wept every day,
	Cinders, poor child, was too hungry to play.
	Slowly they faded and one Summer's night
	Found Mother's features all faded and white;
	Then with big tears slowly dropping I said,
	"Father's a Drunkard, and Mother is dead!"

The Baron falls on his knees before Cinderella

Cinderella and the Trio	Mother, oh! why did you leave me (her) alone?
	With no-one to love me (her), no friends and no home?
	Dark is the night, and the storm rages wild,
	God pity Cinders, the Drunkard's lone child!

Cinderella takes the Baron's hands between hers

Cinderella	Oh! if the Temp'rance men only could find
	Poor wretched Father, and talk very kind—

If they could stop him from drinking—why then
I should be so very happy again!
Is it too late? "Men of Temp'rance", please try,
Or poor little Cinders may soon starve and die.
All the day long I've been begging for bread—
Father's a Drunkard, and Mother is dead!

The Baron staggers off

Cinderella Mother, oh! why did you leave me (her) alone?
and the Trio With no-one to love me (her), no friends and no home?
Dark is the night, and the storm rages wild,
God pity Cinders, the Drunkard's lone child!

The Trio exit. Buttons enters

Buttons (*to the audience*) Hello, kids!
Audience Hello, Buttons!
Buttons Hello, Cindy. Have you finished those spuds yet?
Cinderella Goodness, no. There are so many.
Buttons Well, you'd better hustle. Your stepsisters are screaming their heads off.
Cinderella Did you tell Papa about the broker's men?
Buttons Of course. But what can he do? They're sure to find their way here sooner or later.
Cinderella Poor Papa!

The ugly sisters burst in

Snowdrop Cinderella! Was that you singing?
Cinderella Yes, Snowdrop.
Snowdrop How dare you! How dare you raise your voice in song when your poor thick-headed, flat-footed, broad-fisted, narrow-chested father can't even raise the rent! And what about my booties? Are they polished?
Tulip Ooh, look! She's done *these*! Whose are these? (*She approaches boots*)
Audience Don't touch!!
Tulip Ooh! What nasty noisy nippers!
Snowdrop (*to Cinderella*) Here! Have you peeled the spuds yet?
Tulip And desecrated the carrots?
Snowdrop Is that all you've done?
Tulip Wasting time gossiping with Buttons again!
Snowdrop Well there's not enough here, so *you*'ll have to go without your dinner!
Tulip Yes, and after you've gone without your dinner you can scrub the floor!
Snowdrop And dust the mantelpiece!
Tulip And polish the silver!
Snowdrop And chop the wood!
Tulip And beat the carpets!
Snowdrop And clean our boots!!!

Part I, Scene 5

Tulip The windows are filthy!
Snowdrop The stairs are a disgrace! Look! Look at that! I can write my name in the dust!
Buttons Isn't education wonderful?
Cinderella But I've been cleaning your rooms and making your beds.
Snowdrop Excuses!
Tulip Cheek!
Snowdrop Have you carried up the water for my bath yet?
Cinderella Not yet.
Snowdrop What are you waiting for? Go and do it!
Cinderella Yes, Snowdrop.

Cinderella exits

Buttons I'll help you, Miss Cindy.
Snowdrop You stay here! She's old enough to carry a few buckets of water upstairs.

The Baron enters with Dandini

Baron Ah, there you are, my own dear, sweet, blithering idiots. I can't seem to find my watch. Has anyone seen my watch? Where's Cinderella?
Snowdrop Don't mention that name! (*She stamps her foot*)
Tulip Don't mention that name! (*She stamps on Snowdrop's foot*)
Baron We have a visitor, my dears. (*Aside*) Don't let him see you all at once! (*To Dandini*) Get 'em at this angle. Bit saucy, eh? What *did* I do with that watch?
Snowdrop (*curtsying*) Oh, your Princeship!
Tulip (*likewise*) Your Flagship!
Baron You've met already? (*To Dandini*) Condolences!
Snowdrop Forgive us, me lud, we were not convalescent of your arrival.
Buttons But just a moment, that's not——
Snowdrop You be quiet!
Buttons But——
Snowdrop When we want your opinion we'll give it to you.
Tulip You ought to know better than to talk when she's interrupting.
Baron He has personal invitations from the palace.
Dandini To each of the Baron's family, for the Royal Ball, don't you know.
Buttons Ball?
Snowdrop Ball!
Tulip Ball!!
Baron Three balls! Of course! That's what I did with my watch!
Dandini (*reading card, and handing it to Snowdrop*) "Miss Snowdrop"!
Snowdrop (*curtsying*) Oh, your Princeship!
Dandini "Miss Tulip"! (*He hands her a card*)
Tulip (*curtysing*) Your Flagship!
Snowdrop We thank thee for thy steamed irritation!
Tulip Pardon our consumption!
Snowdrop An honour!
Tulip A pleasure!

Snowdrop Delighted!
Tulip An honour!
Snowdrop I *said* an honour!
Dandini And "Miss Cinderella"!
Snowdrop⎫
Tulip ⎭ (*together, aghast*) Cinderella!!!
Buttons I'll fetch her.
Snowdrop Fetch Cinders? Are you mad?
Buttons She's one of the family!
Tulip One of the family indeed!
Snowdrop She'll shame us!
Tulip Disgrace us!
Baron I'll take her card for now. (*He takes it from Dandini*)
Buttons But Baron, isn't Miss Cindy going to the Ball?
Baron Well, I . . .
Snowdrop Going to the Ball?!!! How *can* she go to the Ball? She has no dresses to wear.
Tulip Unless she goes as a rag doll!
Snowdrop Or a tramp!
Tulip Or a scarecrow!

They laugh uproariously

Snowdrop (*to Dandini*) A family joke, your Princeship. You wouldn't get it! (*She pushes him playfully*)

Polly rushes in

Baron Ah, Polly, my little niece, what is it?
Polly Uncle! Uncle! The broker's men are coming! They just asked me if this was your house!
Baron Oh heaven help me! What's to be done?
Tulip What's to be done??
Snowdrop Six months!
Tulip Who's to do 'em?
Snowdrop Pa!
Buttons Why not offer them your automobile as part payment?
Baron How can I? I'm still paying instalments on the automobile I swapped for the automobile I traded in as a part exchange on the automobile I'm ten payments behind on now!

A loud doorknock off L

Snowdrop Quick! Hide everything!

During the following dialogue they pull the large skip downstage to beside the entrance R, *and open it. From around the room they collect the following articles and place them into the skip: Buttons puts the chair in, Polly fetches two large candlesticks from the mantelpiece, Dandini gets a clock. Snowdrop and Tulip go to the cupboard from where Snowdrop takes out a fan, and Tulip a parcel which she unwraps*

Part I, Scene 5

Buttons Oh, it's a moving sight, a moving sight!
Baron What is?
Buttons Watching the bailiffs taking your furniture away!
Snowdrop Oh, me most precious possession!
Tulip What is it?
Snowdrop (*crossing to the skip*) I once went on tour with *Lady Windermere's Fan*, and I never gave it back! (*She drops it in the skip*)
Tulip What's this?
Snowdrop Oooooh! We must save that. That's the Sunday joint!
Tulip The butcher gave you a lot of fat, didn't he? (*She gives the joint to Snowdrop*)
Snowdrop That's what you think! I had to pay for it! (*She drops the joint into the skip*)

The old "Victorian" telephone on the wall rings. The Baron pulls the complete box off the wall and rushes to the skip with it

Polly Whatever's that, Baron?
Baron It's a telephone!
Polly A telephone!?
Snowdrop New-fangled contraptions!
Tulip (*picking up a large pair of colourful ladies' drawers full of holes in the seat and legs*) I always wanted to wear long pants. But I didn't want to wear them this long! (*She drops them into the skip*)
Snowdrop Where's me musical instrument? (*She takes out a potty from the cupboard*)
Baron What sort of musical instrument do you call that?
Snowdrop (*crossing to the skip*) Never heard of chamber music? (*She drops it into the skip*)

Another loud doorknock off L

Polly Hurry!
Baron Quick, the tablecloth!

Buttons and Polly take the large red chequered tablecloth from the table and drape it over the skip. The Baron places a vase containing one flower on it. Loud knock off L

Hide!

They all squeeze under the table, with Dandini and Buttons at either end. Another knock off L

Cinderella enters R

Cinderella Father, there is someone at the door. (*As she can see no-one, she crosses to the exit* L) Who can it be? (*She exits*)
Tulip Oh, that stupid Cinderella!
Buttons It's not her fault!
Cinderella (*off*) Oh!
Wormwood (*off*) Aha!

Scrubbs (*off*) Aha!

Wormwood and Scrubbs enter, followed by Cinderella

Wormwood We've come for the money.
Scrubbs We've come for the money.
Cinderella But we have no money.
Wormwood Then we'll take the furniture and effects!
Scrubbs The furniture and effects!
Wormwood (*to Scrubbs*) We'll start with the effects!
Scrubbs Effects, right! (*Shouting off*) Effects!!

There is a loud burst of wind, galloping horse, gunshots, motor horns, steam trains, and a woman screaming, each effect merging rapidly into the next

Wormwood Not sound effects, you Charlie! (*He crosses to the skip*)
Scrubbs Oh, sorry! (*He takes out a notebook and pencil*)
Wormwood (*picking up a vase*) One vaise, vass, or vawse, with flower.
Scrubbs (*writing in the book*) One vaise, vass, or vawse, with flower.
Wormwood (*gathering up the cloth*) One cloth—table.
Scrubbs One cloth, table.

The telephone rings inside the skip

Wormwood (*opening the skip*) Ah—ha!
Scrubbs Ah—ha!
Baron Ooh—hoo!
Others Ssssssh!

Scrubbs exits R with the tablecloth and vase, and returns during the following

Dandini and Buttons rise, and come downstage to Wormwood

Dandini Can we be of assistance, old sport?
Buttons There's a lot to carry.
Wormwood Right!

Wormwood stands behind the skip, Buttons to his right, and Scrubbs on Buttons' right

Dandini exits. At least one Stagehand will be needed to stand by between Scrubbs at the DR entrance and Dandini who appears at the window UR and will pass the props back in through the window

Wormwood takes the articles out of the skip one-by-one and passes them to Buttons who passes them to Scrubs who passes them to the Stagehand in the wings who passes them to Dandini. Wormwood, Buttons and Scrubbs call out each item as they pass it along the line. The Baron, Polly, Cinderella, Tulip and Snowdrop form a chain diagonally across the stage between the window UR and the cupboard L. Dandini passes the articles back in through the window to the Baron and they proceed along the line to Snowdrop, who piles them into the cupboard. The whole scene should move very neatly and swiftly

One pair of candlesticks.

Part I, Scene 5

Buttons One pair of candlesticks.
Scrubbs One pair of candlesticks.
Wormwood One joint.
Buttons That's a Sunday joint.
Wormwood One joint, Sunday for the use of.
Buttons One joint, Sunday for the use of.
Scrubbs One joint, Sunday for the use of.
Wormwood One clock!
Buttons One clock.
Scrubbs One clock.
Wormwood One fan!
Buttons Lady Windermere's!
Wormwood One Lady Windermere's type fan.
Buttons One Lady Windermere type fan.
Scrubbs One Lady Windermere type fan.
Wormwood (*holding up the drawers*) One pair of these!
Buttons One pair of these.
Scrubbs One pair of those!
Wormwood One——?
Buttons Telephone—new fangled.
Wormwood One new-fangled telephone.
Buttons One new-fangled telephone.
Scrubbs One new-fangled telephone.
Wormwood (*holding up the potty*) One of these!
Buttons One of these.
Scrubbs One of those!
Wormwood One chair!
Buttons One chair.
Scrubbs One chair.

Scrubbs exits with the chair

Wormwood (*spying the boots and approaching*) Aha! One pair of——
Audience Don't touch!!
Wormwood (*consulting his notebook*) Oh yes! I've got a note of that! (*He ticks his notebook*) Now then, where next?

Buttons distracts his attention from upstage where, as soon as the chair is passed through, the Baron, Polly, Cinderella, Tulip and Snowdrop hide under the table again

Buttons You've got a difficult job here.
Wormwood Yes, oh yes!
Buttons Tell me, how many work in your firm?
Wormwood About one in ten!
Buttons Oh?

Wormwood begins to turn upstage

(*Distracting him*) What do the others do all day?
Wormwood Nothing.
Buttons How do they know when they've finished?

Scrubbs enters

Wormwood You ready?
Buttons (*to Scrubbs*) How long you been with the firm?
Scrubbs Fifty-five years.
Buttons *Fifty-five years?*
Scrubbs Fifty-five years.
Buttons How old are you?
Scrubbs Forty-five!
Buttons Wait a minute, how did you manage that?
Scrubbs Overtime!

The telephone rings in the cupboard

Wormwood Cupboard!
Scrubbs Cupboard!

They cross to the cupboard. Wormwood takes out the articles and passes them to Buttons who passes them to Scrubbs who passes them to a Stagehand at the DL *entrance. The procedure is the same as before, but this time Dandini is at the window* UL *and the Baron, Polly, Cinderella, Tulip and Snowdrop form a line between that window and the chest* UR, *with Snowdrop taking the articles from Dandini and the Baron packing them into the chest*

Wormwood One vaise, vass, or vawse, with flower.
Buttons One vaise, vass, or vawse, with flower.
Scrubbs One vaise, vass, or vawse, with flower.
Wormwood One cloth—table.
Buttons One cloth—table.
Scrubbs One cloth—table.
Wormwood One pair of candlesticks.
Buttons One pair of candlesticks.
Scrubbs One pair of candlesticks.
Wormwood One joint, Sunday for the use of.
Buttons One joint, Sunday for the use of.
Scrubbs One joint, Sunday for the use of.
Wormwood One clock.
Buttons One clock.
Scrubbs One clock.
Wormwood One Lady Windermere type fan.
Buttons One Lady Windermere type fan.
Scrubbs One Lady Windermere type fan.
Wormwood (*holding up the drawers*) One pair of these.
Buttons One pair of these.
Scrubbs One pair of those!
Wormwood One new-fangled telephone!

The telephone rings. Buttons answers it

Buttons Hello? . . . (*To Wormwood*) It's for you. It's from Manchester.
Wormwood Hello? Manchester? . . . What's the weather like down there?

A jet of water shoots out of the mouthpiece, hitting Wormwood in the face

Scrubbs That line's been tapped!
Buttons One new-fangled telephone!
Scrubbs One new-fangled telephone!
Wormwood (*holding up the potty*) One of these!
Buttons One of these!
Scrubbs One of those!
Wormwood One chair!
Buttons One chair.
Scrubbs One chair!

When Dandini has passed the chair to Snowdrop, he climbs through the window and joins the others, who, this time, do not hide but stand well upstage, watching

Buttons (*business with Wormwood as before*) I like your mate. He must be very useful to you.
Wormwood He was nothing till he met me. Nothing!
Buttons Is that so?
Wormwood Nothing. A ragamuffin!
Buttons You don't say?
Wormwood His hair was so long he used to get dandruff in his socks!
Buttons That's not good.
Wormwood And his clothes! He used to step off the pavement straight into his pocket! And lazy!
Buttons Was he lazy?
Wormwood He was so lazy he married a widow with five children!
Buttons How is he with old ladies?
Wormwood I'll tell you. There was this old lady, see, standing in Rose Street. Oscar rushes up to her, all out of breath, and asks if she's seen a policeman about anywhere. She says "no".
Buttons So?
Wormwood So he bashes her over the head and pinches her handbag.
Buttons Her handbag!
Wormwood Yes, he said he thought the change would do him good!
Buttons But he's all right now?
Wormwood Oh, yes, he's all right now.
Scrubbs I'm all right now.

The telephone rings inside the chest

Wormwood The chest!
Scrubbs The chest!

Without noticing the others, Wormwood, Buttons and Scrubbs cross in front of them to the chest. Wormwood passes the articles to Buttons who passes them to Scrubbs who passes them to the Baron, and so on, so that they go directly back into the cupboard. As before, Wormwood, Buttons and Scrubbs call out the items as they pass them along

Wormwood One vaise!
Buttons One vass!

Scrubbs One vawse!
Wormwood One cloth—table!

Buttons and Scrubbs repeat each article after Wormwood as they pass them, now very quickly, along the line

> One pair candlesticks! One joint, Sunday for the use of! One clock! One Lady Windermere type fan! One pair of these! One new-fangled telephone! One of these! One chair!

As the others finish passing the chair, they step back to level with the upstage wall so that Wormwood doesn't notice them

> That's about the lot then. (*He produces a form and pencil*) Sign 'ere!

Buttons signs

> And 'ere ... And 'ere!

Wormwood crosses towards the exit L, *notices the cupboard, looks in, closes the cupboard door and double-takes. The telephone rings and he looks in again*

Ah—ha!
Scrubbs (*beside him*) Ah—ha!

The others form a line between the cupboard and the skip and pass the articles accordingly, with Wormwood calling them out and Buttons and Scrubbs repeating them as before

Wormwood (*very quickly*) One vaise, one cloth—table, one pair candlesticks, one joint, Sunday for the use of, one clock, one Lady Windermere type fan, one pair of these, one new-fangled telephone, one of those, one chair!

Wormwood leans against the cupboard until the others have finished, then he crosses to the chest and looks in. The others follow him. He sighs happily. The others sigh too. The telephone rings. He double-takes—and removes the articles. This time the others replace the articles in their original positions—the candlesticks to the mantelpiece, the chair by the fire, the telephone on the wall, the fan, joint and potty in the cupboard, etcetera, etcetera. The items are called out as before

> One vaise, one cloth—table, one pair candlesticks, one joint, Sunday for the use of, one clock, one Lady Windermere type fan, one pair of these, one new-fangled telephone, one of those, one chair!!!

Wormwood faints with exhaustion and collapses neatly into the skip. Snowdrop pushes Scrubbs's chest and he also collapses into the skip. They close the lid, cover it with the cloth and put the vase containing the flower on it

> Dandini, Buttons, Polly and the Baron wheel the skip off

Snowdrop Well, that's got rid of them! Look at the mess they've made. Cinders, you'll have to clear it up, while we're having dinner—and be quick!

Tulip You can begin by scrubbing the floor. Here! (*She hands Cinderella a bucket and cloth*)
Cinderella Yes, Tulip. (*She goes down on her knees and begins to wash the floor*)
Snowdrop Look at her, the little urchin! Can you imagine her at a Ball?
Tulip Not unless she went as a rag-doll!

The ugly sisters begin to exit

Snowdrop Or a tramp!
Tulip Or a scarecrow!

The ugly sisters go

Cinderella on her knees, washing the floor. She begins to cry

Cinderella I mustn't cry! I mustn't . . . I don't know why they are so unkind to me. I do all I can to please them.

Fairy Flora enters disguised as the old woman

Am I really so ugly? Is there no-one in the world who can love me? (*She sees the old woman*) Oh, it's you!
Flora I wish you well. Pray have no fears,
Sweet Cinderella, dry your tears.
I may be of help, I think;
But first *please* give me food—and drink!
Cinderella Why, of course, old dame. (*She gives her a piece of bread from a pocket in her apron*) This is all I have I'm afraid. If you'll come out to the well I'll get you some water. But please be quick. My sisters will be back soon, and they will be angry with me if they find me giving food.
Flora No, never fear, they'll not return—
Your sisters are of no concern;
I wish to speak with only you.
Please finish what you have to do.
(*She raises her arm as if casting a spell*)
Cinderella (*returning to her floor washing*) Yes, I must get on with my work . . . I feel so drowsy . . . and I have so . . . much to . . . do. I can hardly . . . keep my eyes open . . . I'm . . . so . . . tired. (*She sleeps*)
Flora Sleep, Cinderella! Now I see
The way you're treated by these three—
You must work so they can play.
For this, their cruelty shall pay!
Though you take me for another
I am your Fairy Godmother!
(*She reveals herself as Fairy Flora*)
By our Fairy Chancery
Entrusted to watch over thee.

Song No. 9 Let Me Kiss Her For Her Mother
By John P. Ordway and L. O. Emerson

Flora sings, accompanied by the Chorus, off

Flora and
Chorus (*off*) Let us kiss her for her mother,
Let us kiss her youthful brow;
We will love her for her mother,
And give our blessing now.
Though cold that form lies sleeping,
She wears an angel's crown;
Kind friends unseen are weeping
And lay her gently down.

Sleep, dearest, sleep,
We love you as no other,
Kind friends around you weep,
We kiss you for your mother.

Black-out

Scene 6

The ugly sisters' boudoir. (Third stage)

Buttons enters with two chairs

Buttons Hello, kids!
Audience Hello, Buttons!

Buttons places the chairs upstage

  Snowdrop enters in her underwear

Snowdrop Buttons! Buttons! Where are they! Are they here?
Buttons Who?
Snowdrop The Beauty Specialists!
Buttons Beauty Specialists!!!

  Tulip enters in her underwear and wearing a hat

Tulip Are they here? Are they here?
Snowdrop Not yet! (*She sees the hat*) What have you got on your head?
Tulip It's the latest model.
Snowdrop That's not a model, it's a horrible example.
Tulip Don't be catty. It makes me feel better. Whenever I'm down in the dumps I always get myself a new hat.
Snowdrop I wondered where you got them! What dress are you going to wear?
Tulip I'm going as the Sugar Plum Fairy.
Snowdrop Thank heavens for that. (*To Buttons*) I was afraid she might wear her biblical gown.

Part I, Scene 6

Buttons Her biblical gown?
Snowdrop (*gesturing*) Low and behold! I'm going as Little Bo-Peep!

Doorbell

Snowdrop ⎫
Tulip   ⎬ (*together*) It's them!
Snowdrop Let them in, Buttons.

Buttons exits

Now you, don't forget these beauticians are very select. So when it's all over don't ask for the bill!
Tulip What do I ask for?
Snowdrop You ask for the William!

The broker's men enter wearing artist's smocks. Wormwood sports a beard, a chic beret, and a cigarette holder. Scrubbs has a bright blonde wig. They are both very camp. Scrubbs pushes a little handcart, the sides of which bear the device:

WORMWOOD & SCRUBBS
Beauty Parlour
(Heavy division)

Wormwood *Bonjour, bonjour, bonjour!* (*He kisses Snowdrop's hand*)
Scrubbs Kkkkk—kkkkk! Allo! Allo! Kkkk—kkkkk! (*He kisses Snowdrop's hand*)
Snowdrop Oh, I say, French! How do you do.
Wormwood My name's Stanley, and this is my friend, Pebbles!
Scrubbs Kkkk—kkk! Ow-do-you-do! Kkkkk—kkkkk!
Snowdrop You look a bit red in the face—have you got a temperature?
Scrubbs Kkkkk! Beg pardon?
Snowdrop You seem a bit flushed. Have you flu'?
Scrubbs (*forgetting the French accent*) Oh no, we walked here! (*He remembers*) Kkkkk—kkkk!
Snowdrop (*to Wormwood*) He speaks very good English. Where did he learn it?
Wormwood On an Edison Phonograph!
Scrubbs Kkkkk—kkkkk!
Snowdrop Oh, I see.
Wormwood Shall we commence?

Scrubbs takes a spade out of the cart

Snowdrop Here, what's that for?
Wormwood A beautiful woman is like a beautiful garden—they both need a good dig from time to time!

During the following, they take a cloth from the cart and spread it on the ground. The ugly sisters place the chairs on it side by side and sit. The broker's men produce caps and covers, which they place on the ugly sisters. Then they each take out a bowl of liquid mud

Snowdrop Now do a good job, boys. We want to look beautiful.
Tulip Yes, we want to look ravished!
Wormwood Don't worry, you will!
Snowdrop We're going to a very posh do.
Wormwood Fancy!
Tulip It's so posh that even though they've got *saucers*, we still have to drink out of the cups!
Wormwood Well, get you!
Tulip We might find a husband there!
Snowdrop What do you mean, *we* might?

Wormwood and Scrubbs now go to Snowdrop and Tulip respectively, slosh on the mud and begin to massage their faces

Tulip Mind my ears!
Snowdrop Yes, mind her ears. She's got dust-pan ears.
Wormwood Dust-pan ears?
Snowdrop They pick up all the dirt!
Tulip Oooooh! I've got a pain in my tummy!
Wormwood (*medicine salesman*) Ladies! Do you suffer from pains in the stomach? Do you suffer from flatulence? Heartburn? Indigestion? You do? Then why not do what thousands of others do? (*He belches*)
Tulip I think I need something for my liver.
Scrubbs She needs something for her liver.
Snowdrop Give her a pound of onions!
Tulip Ooooh, you cat! (*She scrapes off a handful of mud and flings it at Snowdrop*)
Snowdrop Don't you start, you little hooligan! (*She flings some back*)

Short mud battle

Wormwood Ladies! Ladies! Please! Right Pebbles, darling! Towels!

They clean off the mud

No, I've always found that the old-fashioned remedies are the best.
Snowdrop Don't talk to me about old-fashioned remedies.
Wormwood Oh?
Snowdrop Thanks to the old-fashioned remedy of soaking me feet in vinegar, I've now got pickled bunions!

She continues to talk, but Wormwood massages and slaps her face so vigorously that we can't understand a word she says. He ends by wrapping a towel round her head and face, so only a muffled moaning is heard

Scrubbs (*at the end of all this*) Are you troubled with bad dreams?
Tulip No, I rather enjoy them.

Buttons enters

Buttons Howdy, kids!
Audience Howdy, Buttons!

Scrubbs gets the powder from the handcart

Buttons Miss Tulip?
Tulip What is it?
Buttons Miss Cindy says your dress is ready.
Tulip (*leaping out of the chair*) Oooooh! Do you hear that, Snowdrop? Me dress is ready! Whoopeeee!

Tulip makes a wild gesture of delight, and knocks Scrubbs's hand containing a thickly-laden powder puff into his face covering him with powder

Tulip rushes off, followed by Buttons

Wormwood Make-up!
Scrubbs Make-up! (*He takes a make-up tray from the cart and stands by Wormwood*)
Snowdrop Oh, goodygumdrops!
Wormwood Lip-rouge!
Scrubbs Lip-rouge! (*He passes it to him like a nurse attending an operation*)

Wormwood draws large lips on Snowdrop

Wormwood Eyebrow tweezers!
Scrubbs Eyebrow tweezers! (*He hands Wormwood an enormous pair of pincers*)
Snowdrop (*as they are applied*) Ooooh! Ow! Eeeh! Ow!
Wormwood Eyebrow pencil.
Scrubbs Eyebrow pencil.

Wormwood draws eyebrows

Wormwood Eye shadow!
Scrubbs Eye shadow!

Wormwood daubs blue above the eyes

Wormwood Mascara!
Scrubbs Mascara!

Wormwood draws black lines around the eyes

Wormwood Powder!
Scrubbs Powder!

Scrubbs hands Wormwood the powder, puts the tray down, and prepares for the next business. Wormwood covers Snowdrop with clouds of powder and tries to comb her hair

Wormwood Hello, hello, What *have* we here, madam? Dandruff?
Snowdrop Just a few chips off the old block.
Wormwood Singe!!
Scrubbs Singe! (*He lights a taper*)
Snowdrop (*seeing a taper*) Hey! What's this? What's this? What's this?
Wormwood Just a singe!
Snowdrop Oh! I thought he was going to start hunting for them with a flame-thrower!

Wormwood (*to Scrubbs*) Never mind!
Scrubbs How about some of this? It'll make you nice and brown.
Snowdrop What is it?
Scrubbs Gravy!
Snowdrop I'll manage without, thank you.

Scrubbs replaces the taper and jar

Wormwood Wig!
Scrubbs Wig!

Buttons enters with Snowdrop's Ball wig

Buttons Hello, kids!
Audience Hello, Buttons!

Buttons hands the wig to Scrubbs, and exits

Scrubbs hands it to Wormwood, who places it on Snowdrop's head

Wormwood Our very latest creation—"The Madame Pompadour"!
Snowdrop Looks more like the coal-house door!
Wormwood Corsets!!
Scrubbs Corsets!

Buttons enters with the corsets. They have hooks and eyes down the front and tightening cords at the back

Buttons Hello, kids!
Audience Hello, Buttons!
Buttons Corsets! (*He hands them to Scrubbs*)
Scrubbs Corsets! (*He hands them to Wormwood*)
Wormwood (*struggling to fit them on to Snowdrop*) You know, you ought to go on a diet.
Snowdrop What do you mean?
Wormwood You ought to eat nuts. They're good for the figure.
Snowdrop Nuts?!
Wormwood You've never seen a monkey wearing corsets!
Scrubbs (*studying Snowdrop*) Oh, I don't know...
Snowdrop You be quiet!

Scrubbs puts the props back into the cart

Wormwood I can't do this bottom one up!
Scrubbs I know. Nobody can!

Song No. 10

Snowdrop, Buttons, Wormwood and Scrubbs sing

After the second verse the Stage Manager enters with the words of the chorus on an easel and exits with the chairs

Buttons joins Wormwood and Scrubbs and they struggle to pull the two cords tight at the back of Snowdrop's corsets as they sing the chorus with the audience. *They give up struggling with the corset and Wormwood and Scrubbs sing the next verse, resuming their struggle as everyone joins with the audience in the last chorus*

   At the end of the number Cinderella enters with Snowdrop's "Little Bo-Peep" costume

The broker's men roll up the cloth and tidy up

Cinderella Here you are, Snowdrop. I've finished your dress.
Snowdrop About time too. Help me on with it.

Buttons and Cinderella help her into the dress

Buttons (*as they dress her*) Miss Snowdrop, I've been thinkin'.
Snowdrop I thought you'd gone a bit pale!
Buttons You've got lots of dresses. Why don't you lend Miss Cindy one of yours?
Snowdrop What on earth for?
Buttons So she can go to the Ball.
Cinderella I'd take great care of it, Snowdrop.
Snowdrop Certainly not! If you can't think of anything better than that, you'd better not think! How do I look?
Wormwood Heaven, darling!
Scrubbs Like you said—ravished!

Tulip enters as the "Sugar Plum Fairy"

Tulip Here I am! Here I am!
Snowdrop What the 'eck's that supposed to be?
Tulip The Sugar Plum Fairy!
Snowdrop You look as if Little Jack Horner's been at you!
Wormwood Well, if you don't mind, we'll settle and toddle.
Snowdrop Oh, must you? Well, you'd better come and have a word with Papa. (*She crosses to exit*) You may find him a bit short of tin, but perhaps you'd settle for a sack of All-Bran?
Wormwood How gay! I've always wanted to be a *regular* coiffeur!

Wormwood and Snowdrop exit

Tulip Age before beauty!
Scrubbs Muck before the shovel!
Tulip Oh, thank you!

Tulip exits, followed by Scrubbs wheeling his cart

Cinderella Oh Buttons! I shall never get to the Ball now.
Buttons Don't give up, Miss Cindy. We've got one more chance. You haven't asked the Baron yet. He'll let you go for sure.
Cinderella I don't know.
Buttons (*taking her hand*) Well come on! We'll ask him!

The cloth rises behind them, and they are in the kitchen again

Scene 7

The kitchen in Hardup Hall (fullstage)
The Baron is pacing up and down impatiently

Baron (*shouting*) Snowdrop! Tulip! Come along—we're going to be late! It's a foolish thing, asking me to go to a Ball. I don't dance. The only way *I* care for hops is in a liquid state! Ah, Cinderella! What are your sisters *doing* for heaven's sake?
Cinderella They're nearly ready, Papa.
Baron And what are those boots doing there? Can't you keep this place a bit tidy? (*He approaches the boots*)
Audience Don't touch!
Baron Oh yes, I forgot! I'm sure we shouldn't go to this Ball. I'm sure it's a mistake. If only I were rich like the Baron of Bloxwich.
Buttons He may be rich, but they say he's cracked.
Baron He may be cracked, but he's not broke!
Cinderella Papa, why can't I have fine clothes and be dressed up and look like my sisters?
Baron I don't know, my dear. There's a special knack in looking like your sisters.
Buttons A poor look-out for Barnum and Bailey if we were all freaks! But Baron, sir, have you got Miss Cindy's invitation card?
Baron Oh, yes ... Why, here it is. (*He gives it to Cinderella*)
Buttons Then she can go too, sir, can't she?
Baron Well, I don't know ... it's her sisters, you see, they say ...
Buttons But what do *you* say, Baron?
Baron Well, *I* don't see why ...

Snowdrop bursts in followed by Tulip who holds one hand delicately to her forehead

Snowdrop Now then! Now then! What's all this?
Cinderella Oh, Snowdrop, I do want to go to the Ball so very much.
Snowdrop You're not still on about that, are you?
Buttons She's got an invitation card just like you!
Snowdrop (*snatching the card away from Cinderella*) Oh *has* she? (*She tears it into four pieces*) Well now she hasn't got an invitation card!
Cinderella Oh!
Tulip No! Now she's got four! (*She gurgles with glee, then holds her head again*) Ohhh!
Snowdrop Cheek! If it weren't for taking off me velvet glove and hexposing me diamond ring to the hatmosphere, I'd slap her saucy face! Are you ready, Papa?
Baron Yes, my dear.
Snowdrop And about time! Come on! (*Crossing to the exit; to Cinderella*) And while we're gone you just finish cleaning up this house. It's a disgrace!
Tulip I've got a terrible headache. Terrible!

Part I, Scene 7

Baron Headache? Have you, my pet?
Snowdrop She was putting some toilet-water on her hair and the seat fell down on her head. Come on!

Snowdrop, Tulip, and the Baron exit

Cinderella bursts into tears. Buttons takes her into his arms, and comforts her

Buttons Never you mind, Miss Cindy. Don't cry. You don't want to go to that rotten old Ball anyway. (*He sits Cinderella by the fire*)
Cinderella But I do! I do (*She sobs quietly*)
Buttons Please don't cry, Miss Cindy. (*He tries to think of a way to cheer her up. He takes out a bag of sweets and offers her one*) Gobstopper!

Cinderella shakes her head

(*Holding out his hand upside down, the fingers half-curled and taut*) Look! What's that?
Cinderella I don't know. What is it?
Buttons A dead one of those! (*He holds his hand the right way up*)

Cinderella continues to sob

All right then, you shall go to the Ball. We'll both go!
Cinderella Oh Buttons, how can we?
Buttons We'll go to our own Ball!
Cinderella Where?
Buttons At my palace of course. (*He turns the table upside down and arranges the chairs*) My second palace, naturally. I never use my best palace for Balls.
Cinderella Buttons, are you feeling all right?
Buttons I shall go dressed as a caterpillar—and so must you!
Cinderella A caterpillar?? I'd rather go as a butterfly!
Buttons (*shocked*) Certainly not! No butterflies allowed!
Cinderella Why not?
Buttons It's a moth ball!
Cinderella (*laughing*) Oh Buttons, you are silly!

Buttons puts a chair up to the table so that it resembles a horse and coach, and two other chairs inside the table for carriage seats

Buttons Well, your Highness, are you ready?
Cinderella "Your Highness"! Who am I?
Buttons A princess of course—the most beautiful princess in the land—and I'm your prince. You love me very much ... But our parents won't let us marry.
Cinderella Why not?
Buttons We're still at the awkward age.
Cinderella The awkward age?
Buttons Too old to cry—to young to swear!
Cinderella So what are we to do?
Buttons We'll ignore them and elope. Your Highness, your carriage awaits!

They mime getting into their carriage and driving away. Buttons sings

Song No. 11

At the appropriate moment the Stage Manager enters with the words of the chorus

Buttons and Cinderella sing with the audience. During the chorus Buttons presents Cinderella with a cabbage wrapped up like a bouquet. At the end of the number they both sit in silence for a moment

(*Speaking*) Miss Cindy... there's something I want to tell you... For a long time now I... You know I... Look, I wrote this poem— specially for you... (*He kneels and reads from a piece of paper*)
"My love is like a cabbage, divided into two,
The leaves I give to others, but the heart I give to you."
(*He offers her the paper*)

Cinderella sits with bowed head, trying not to cry

Excuse me, Miss Cindy!

Buttons runs off

Fairy Flora enters, disguised as an old woman

Flora Now Cinderella, why so sad?
There's nothing in the world so bad
A smile can't cure. Whate'er befall
Tonight you *shall* go to the Ball!
Cinderella But who are you to help another?
Flora (*revealing herself*) I am your Fairy Godmother!
Cinderella What miracle is this? What power?
Flora No need to fear, pray do not cower.
Your sisters' evil you withstood
Because you're gentle, pure and good.
Your dearest wish shall now come true.
Come, Fairies, we have work to do!

Attendant Fairies enter

Fetch me a pumpkin, quickly pray!
To take our Princess on her way.

The Fairy exits

Catch me a rat, lizards and mice,
And bring them to me in a trice.

Two more Fairies exit

Cinderella Pumpkin? Lizard? Mice and rat?
But what will be the use of that?
Flora Patience, daughter, all shall be
As promised. You shall see!

Part I, Scene 7

The Fairies return with the pumpkin, rat, lizards and mice, which they place before Flora. Aconite enters

Aconite I warn you once again, rash fairy
  The mystic power in whom there lies,
  Aid not this good and simple maiden
  Whom I desire to ostracize.
Flora You have no power, evil spirit of night,
  Over pumpkin, rat, lizard or mice.
  See how my magic shall make them obey
  And help my godchild in a trice!
Aconite Do not heed her, gentle lizards!
  Nimble rat, she is your foe!
Flora My desire shall be accomplished
  Evil genius! Now go! Go!
Aconite Foolish fairy! You think the day you've won!
  But ere the first glimpse of tomorrow's sun,
  If she should stay beyond the midnight hour
  No help of yours can shield her from my power!

Aconite exits

The Fairy Ballet music begins as the Lights dim to a spot on Fairy Flora

In the darkness, Cinderella is replaced by her stand-in who wears identical clothes. She stands in a fairly obscure position, with her back to the audience, watching the ballet

Flora Let our Fairy Dance begin
  As our magic spell we spin.
  Pumpkin, rat and mice herewith
  All ingredients we give.
  Every elf and fairy sprite
  Bear her to the Ball tonight,
  With our magic fairy power,
  For Cinderella's glorious hour!

The Lights fade up as the Fairies dance a Fairy Ballet. They place the pumpkin, rat, lizards and mice in front of the fireplace

  Now with your fairy spells approach!

The Fairies encircle the pumpkin etc., casting their spells

  Fairy horses! Fairy coach!

There is a bright flash and a Black-out

Now wearing a beautiful ballroom gown, looking indeed like a princess, the real Cinderella replaces her stand-in. The fireplace disappears and in its place is set a beautiful fairy coach complete with horses, a coachman and liveried footmen (who replace mice, rat and lizard)

The Lights snap on again

Cinderella It's beautiful! What can I say?
Flora Your coach, your Highness! Enter pray!
Cinderella Oh, thank you! And the Royal Ball?
May I go there after all?
Flora You may. Our magic fairy power
Will last until the midnight hour.
But after midnight strikes beware!
Your fairy clothes will disappear—
Your coach and horses be no more—
All will be as it was before.
Be warned!
Cinderella   I will!
Flora   Such is the spell.
Till midnight, God-daughter! Farewell.

One of the Fairies gives Cinderella a large, sparkling invitation card. Cinderella enters the coach

Song No. 12 Fairy Daughter By Heaven Blessed

This is set to the Trio and Finale from Faust *by Charles Gounod, beginning at Mephistopheles' "Quittons—ce lieu sombre, le jour est leve"*

Aconite enters and sings

Aconite	Beware, Fairy Flora! Your spells are in vain!
	Beware the powers of Darkness—the dread midnight
	hour—shall see my revenge!
	The dread midnight hour!
	The world shall behold her disgrace!
Flora	Away! Thou fiend away!
Aconite	Beware!
Flora	Away! Foul demon away!
Aconite	Call back your child, ere 'tis too late
	to save her
Flora	Fairy Daughter, by Heaven bless'd,
	Our faith in thee shall ever rest,
	Remember—ne'er forget I implore thee,
	Those hours—safely that lay before thee.
	Fairy Daughter, by Heaven blessed,
	Our faith in thee shall ever rest!
Aconite	Revenge! Revenge! Shall be mine!
Flora	Fairy Daughter, by Heaven blessed,
	Our faith in thee shall ever rest!
Aconite	Sweet revenge!
Flora	Coachman,

Part I, Scene 7

Flora	take her forth do discover—
Aconite	My curse on her!
Flora	The true one—who will love her forever!
Aconite	I swear revenge!
Flora	To my command—give ear—I pray thee.
Aconite	I swear revenge!—For my hour is near!
Flora and Chorus	Fairy Daughter—by Heaven bless'd
Aconite	Then away! Then away! My dawn is grey!
Flora	Our faith in thee shall ever rest.
Aconite	Then away!—My dawn is grey!
Flora	Remember—ne'er forget I implore—thee
Aconite	Then away!—Then away!
Flora	Those hours—safely that lay before thee.
Aconite	—Oh how I abhor thee!!!
Flora	Fairy Daughter—by Heaven bless'd
Aconite	Then away!—Then away!—My dawn is grey—
Flora	Our faith in thee shall ever rest!
Aconite	Till that the maid's by me possessed!

The wheels of the coach turn, the music swells triumphantly as——

—the CURTAIN *falls*

Alternative ending to Part I

One of the Fairies gives Cinderella a large, sparkling invitation card. Cinderella enters the coach, the wheels of the coach begin to turn and the music of "The Waltz of the Snowflakes", from The Nutcracker Suite *by Tchaikovsky. swells triumphantly. The Chorus hum as a "humming chorus" and Flora sings a verse of Song 3*

CURTAIN

PART II

Scene 8

Outside the palace (frontcloth)

There is a Victorian vintage automobile C. *The Baron is under it attempting repairs, Tulip is leaning against it at one end, and Snowdrop is trying to hitch-hike*

As the Curtain *rises we hear another automobile approaching in the distance. Snowdrop tries desperately to thumb a lift, but it splutters past her with an erratic roar. She tosses her head in disgust. They all sing, to the tune of "John Brown's Body"*

Song No. 13 Our Motor's Broken Down

All
We've been left here stranded in the middle of the road
We've been left here stranded in the middle of the road.
We've been left here stranded in the middle of the road.
'Cos our motor's broken down!

We're waiting for the car-repair man—
To tow us in his car-repair van—
Have you seen the car-repair man?
'Cos our motor's broken down!

Baron I buckled up me bumper on the kerb when I reversed,
There's puncture in the tyre and I think my luck is
      cursed,
I've gone and blown me gasket and me carburettor's
      burst!

All And our motor's broken down!
Now we wish we'd come by hansom,
We *should* have simply called a hansom
If only we had come by hansom—
Or a good old fashioned bus!

Snowdrop Horse-*Bus* conductors hereabouts are most cantankerous.
I saw one turn a fellow off although he made a fuss—
He couldn't pay his fare—and 'twas the driver of the
      bus!
So perhaps we should have walked!

All The traffic's getting worse than ever,
Far too dang'rous altogether,

	It really must affect the weather! Now there's motors *everywhere*!
Tulip	We *all* tried crossing Oxford Street midst many a scream of horn. Across the road a policeman laughed our efforts all to scorn. We asked him how *he* got there—but 'twas there that he was *born*.
All	And our motor's broken down! Where's that bloomin' car-repair man? We're waiting for the car-repair man! Have you seen the car-repair man? 'Cos our motor's broken down!

Tulip (*speaking*) Here comes another one!

Snowdrop starts her thumbing, and again we hear the sound of a car which splutters past them

Snowdrop (*spying Tulip leaning against the automobile*) Here, why should I do all the work? What are you supposed to be doing—holding up the car!
Tulip (*nodding*) Mmmm!
Snowdrop Don't you give me any of your cheek!

Snowdrop drags Tulip away, and the automobile collapses on to the Baron—Tulip has been leaning where one wheel had been removed and was indeed holding up the automobile

Baron Ahhh! Help! Get this off me!

The ugly sisters push the automobile up again, and the Baron crawls out. He and Tulip replace the wheel during the following

Tulip Here comes another one!
Snowdrop Right! I'll make certain this time!

Snowdrop sticks a rose between her teeth, pulls her skirt up above the knee of one leg which she puts forward, and turns herself into a picture of seductiveness. We hear the other automobile approach and putter past. She drops her skirt, flings down the rose and shrugs resignedly. There is a tremendous crash off as the car has hit a tree and smashed to pieces

Serves you right! (*She crosses to watch the others fixing the wheel*) How are you getting on?

A Bear enters, crosses the stage, but stops on seeing the others

Baron Pass me that other spanner, will you?

The Bear picks up the spanner and hands it to him

Thank you!

The Bear continues on its way and exits

Right! Pump!

The ugly sisters fix a pump to the wheel and pump vigorously

The Bear enters, crosses to the wheel at the other end of the car, pulls out the plug and lets the tyre down. There is a loud hiss of escaping air. The Bear exits

Right, that's enough!
Snowdrop So I should hope!
Baron Hello! Well I never! The other one's down. Come on, girls. All hands to the pump!

They cross to the other tyre with the pump

Snowdrop "All hands to the pump", indeed! Ooooh! (*Holding her back*) I feel like a Royal Marine!
Tulip Don't be silly, Snowdrop, where are you going to find a Royal Marine at this time of night?

Snowdrop gives her a withering look. They pump away

The Bear enters and lets down the tyre they have just pumped up. Again there is a loud hiss. The Bear exits

Baron Right, that's enough!
Snowdrop So I should hope! It feels as if me big end's gone!
Tulip Look! That one's down again!
Baron Bless my soul, so it is! As you were, girls!

They cross back to the other tyre

Snowdrop I shall *never* be as I was—ever again!
Baron I can't make it out. These inflatable tyres are the very latest thing!
Tulip Not as late as *we*'re going to be for the Ball!

They are pumping again

The Bear enters and notices the boots which he approaches

Audience Don't touch!

The Bear backs off, surprised, and scratches his head. He goes to the front of the engine and turns the starting handle. The engine starts (recording through a speaker in the automobile). The Bear crosses well downstage of the others as they leap up and climb into the car

Tulip It's going! It's going!
Baron Well bless my soul!
Snowdrop Well come on! Get in! Get in!

They climb in. It is a very small car and a very tight fit. The Bear crosses to the back of the automobile and holds it with one paw, appearing thereby to hold the car back

Well come on, Papa! Get going!
Baron I'm trying to. It won't move!
Snowdrop Won't move? Well pull that plug thing out!

Part II, Scene 8

Snowdrop pulls out the choke. There is a loud explosion (revolver), and the engine stops

The Bear exits

Now what?
Baron I think there's something wrong.
Snowdrop You do surprise me!

They all get out. The Baron raises the bonnet and a giant moth flies out. Tulip grabs a spray-gun from the car and they all chase the moth until it disappears into the wings

That comes of keeping your car in the wardrobe!
Baron Sorry, dear!
Snowdrop You're most eccentric.
Baron (*closing the bonnet*) I think it'll be all right now.

He turns the starting handle, the engine starts, and they all climb in

Snowdrop Now don't travel faster than sound—we want to talk!
Baron (*cheerfully*) Righty-ho! And away we go!

There is a loud explosion and the back falls out. They all fall out backwards on to the floor. The engine stops

The Bear enters and climbs into the automobile

(*As they pick themselves up*) It's no good, girls, I'm afraid we shall have to push it. Come on, girls, noses to the grindstone and shoulders to the wheel!
Snowdrop I know where I'd like to put me foot!

The orchestra plays "John Brown's Body" refrain in dead march time

The Baron, Snowdrop and Tulip push the automobile off. The Bear waves to the audience and toots the horn as they exit

The broker's men enter. Wormwood is dressed as a butcher and Scrubbs as a clown (i.e. the Harlequinade characters) Scrubbs spies the boots and approaches them

Audience Don't touch!
Wormwood Now then, leave them boots alone. They've told you about that before. Well then, here we are!
Scrubbs Here we are.
Wormwood This is the place. Now remember, we want to get a good job in the palace.
Scrubbs A good job in the palace.
Wormwood That's right.
Scrubbs Why?
Wormwood Why?! You want a good job, don't you?
Scrubbs Why?
Wormwood Well, you could earn a lot of money. Maybe a whole pound a week!

Scrubbs Why?
Wormwood Well, then if you saved your money, pretty soon you could open a bank acount. You'd like to have a bank account, wouldn't you?
Scrubbs Why?
Wormwood For heaven's sake! With a big bank account you could retire. You wouldn't have to work any more.
Scrubbs I'm not working now!
Wormwood Never mind that! I don't want you messing everything up like at the last palace we tried to get a job in.
Scrubbs Why do we want to get into the palace anyway?
Wormwood So we can go to the Ball!
Scrubbs Is that why we're dressed up like this?
Wormwood Of course it is, it's a Fancy Dress Ball. You want to go to the Ball, don't you?
Scrubbs I can't dance.
Wormwood There's nothing to it. All you do is turn round and keep wiping your feet!

Scrubbs tries it, circling once on the spot

That's it!
Scrubbs Last time I went to a Fancy Dress Ball I had to go as Atlas.
Wormwood Atlas? Why Atlas?
Scrubbs Somebody pinched me 'at!
Wormwood I don't wish to know that! Look out! Here comes the Major-Domo.
Scrubbs Major what?
Wormwood Domo! Domo!
Scrubbs (*camp*) My dear—and him in the army too!

The Major-Domo enters

Major-Domo (*very camp*) Can I assist you?
Wormwood (*to Scrubbs*) You could be right! (*To the Major-Domo*) We would like to apply for posts in the palace.
Major-Domo What do you do?
Wormwood You've heard of this new, fascinating Japanese Art of Self-Defence?
Major-Domo I think so.
Wormwood Well my friend here is a judi expert.
Major-Domo A judi expert?
Wormwood Oh yes. He's known in the profession as the Kirkcaldy Kid.
Major-Domo He has a talent for pugilism?
Wormwood Oh yes! And he can box too!
Major-Domo Is he good?
Wormwood Good? He's got a wonderful stance! Oscar, show the gentleman your stance.

Scrubbs produces an envelope with stamps

Your stance—not your stamps!

Part II, Scene 8

Scrubbs strikes a boxing attitude

That's it. It's in the family you see. He inherited it all from his father.

Major-Domo (*surveying Scrubbs dubiously*) Hmm! Pity he didn't inherit his father's brains.

Wormwood Oh, he did. But he doesn't get them till he's twenty-one.

Major-Domo I see.

Wormwood Now I suggest that what you need here at the palace is a good bodyguard.

Major-Domo A bodyguard?

Wormwood Imagine! You're sitting all alone by your fireside when some jitsi-jitsi fellow jumps on you from behind. Show him, Oscar!

Scrubbs jumps at the Major-Domo

He jumps on you like that, see?

Major-Domo I see. And throws me? Like that? (*He throws Scrubbs to the floor and puts one foot on his chest*)

Wormwood There you are you see? He's got you down!

Major-Domo He's got *me* down? Who's this then?

Wormwood That's not him. That's you!

Major-Domo Then who's this on top of me?

Wormwood That's the jitsi-jitsi fellow.

Major-Domo (*pointing to Scrubbs*) Then where's he?

Wormwood He's not here. See the danger? See what this jitsi-jitsi fellow does to you? You can't even move your leg.

Major-Domo (*waggling leg*) Oh? What about that?

Wormwood That's not your leg.

Major-Domo (*waggling the other leg*) What about this one then?

Wormwood That's the jitsi-jitsi fellow's leg.

Major-Domo (*shaking Scrubbs' leg*) And this one?

Wormwood How many legs have you got?

The Major-Domo releases Scrubbs, who rises

Major-Domo Yes, I see what you mean.

Wormwood Now, suppose you're strolling up the Grassmarket, and a fellow grabs you by the throat like this. Show him, Oscar!

Scrubbs grabs the Major-Domo by the throat

Major-Domo And throws me like this? (*He throws Scrubbs to the floor as before, and puts his foot on his chest*)

Wormwood Now that couldn't happen if you had a bodyguard.

Major-Domo It just happened to him!

Wormwood He hasn't got a bodyguard!

Major-Domo Ah! So if he were my bodyguard I couldn't get choked like this! (*He chokes Scrubbs*)

Wormwood Exactly!

Major-Domo Or thrown, like this! (*He throws Scrubbs across the stage*)

Wormwood Precisely!

Major-Domo Hmmm! No, I don't think so. He's too short to be a bodyguard!

Wormwood Too short? Right! Wait there! I'll go and get his brother. He's bigger. Come, Oscar!

Wormwood and Scrubbs exit

The Major-Domo sees the boots and approaches them

Audience Don't touch!

The Bear enters, spies the Major-Domo, crosses and stands next to him

The Major-Domo bends his knees, and the Bear copies him. He scratches his head—the Bear does the same. He takes out a cigarette. The Bear produces a box of matches and lights it for him

Major-Domo Thank you. (*He does a double-take, is terrified and begins to sidle nervously towards the exit* L)

Scrubbs and Wormwood return as one man—Scrubbs is on Wormwood's shoulders and wears a very long coat, making him look like a giant

The Major-Domo sees them, is terrified and runs off. The Bear sees them, is also terrified and does the same

Scrubbs and Wormwood follow right across

Scrubbs (*as they go*) I say, did you notice? That Major bloke had a little bear behind?

Scrubbs and Wormwood exit

The orchestra plays. The Lights crossfade to behind the gauze frontcloth, creating a transformation into:

Scene 9

The royal ballroom (full stage)

In a prominent position is a large ornate clock. During the scene the hands move imperceptibly until they arrive at midnight at the appropriate moment. There is a low rostrum right across the back of the stage, with steps leading down from its centre. It has pillars along it rising to the ceiling

The Lights fade up behind the front gauze to reveal a grandiose scene of the royal guests in fancy-dress costumes and masks—in a stationary and frozen tableau. As many recognizable characters as possible should be represented in the costumes—primarily, nursery-rhyme and pantomime characters e.g. Dick Whittington, Robin Hood, Little Red Riding Hood, Humpty Dumpty, etc. etc. The Harlequinade characters are wearing their appropriate costumes

As the gauze is raised the characters become animated and engage in a short, formal dance to the music of "The Grandfather's Dance" from Tchaikovsky's second Nutcracker Suite, *Act I "Grossvater"*

Part II, Scene 9

At the end of the dance the Major-Domo enters and strikes his staff on the floor three times

Major-Domo Pray silence for Her Royal Majesty, Queen Mariana, and His Royal Highness, Prince Charming!

Fanfare off, followed by a short, quaint, national anthem

Queen Mariana and Prince Charming enter

All the Guests bow low as the royal pair proceed to their chairs

The Major-Domo exits

Queen It gives me great pleasure—to welcome you here today—to our Royal Ball—which we are holding here, in our own home. My son and I—are deeply touched—to see so many of you here on this happy occasion—and our welcome goes out to you all—whoever you may be. (*She sits*)

Applause

(*To the Prince*) I nearly wandered off into my ship-launching speech there for a moment!

The Major-Domo enters

Major-Domo Her Royal Highness, Princess Andromeda!
Prince Oh no, Mother!
Queen Your own baby cousin? Why not?
Prince I didn't know the Royal Reformatory had let her out!

Fanfare

Andromeda enters—a large, precocious "little" girl of ten. She sucks a huge lollipop

Andromeda Hello, Auntie! Watcha, Charmers!
Prince Hello, Andy.
Andromeda (*to the Major-Domo*) All right, Tiny Tim, you can beat it!

The Major-Domo exits

Queen Now child, that is not the way to speak to the Major-Domo.
Prince Yes, Andy, watch your tongue.
Andromeda (*squinting*) I can't! My nose is in the way! Scrumptious party, Auntie! I've already had six icecreams!
Queen You've had eight—but who's counting? Enjoy yourself, my dear!

The Major Domo enters

Andromeda (*offering her lollipop to the Prince*) Want a suck?
Prince I'm trying to give them up.
Queen Come and stand by me, child.
Major-Domo His excellency, the Ambassador for Moscow—Olaf Derlottoff!

The Bear enters. All the ladies scream and flee, followed closely by the men, including the Major-Domo

Only the Queen, the Prince, Andromeda and the Bear are left. The Bear removes his head—and it is Dandini

Dandini Well honestly! I don't know what everybody's so jolly frightened about!
Andromeda (*chortling with delight*) Jolly good, Dandy. You scared the pants off them!
Prince Dandini, you are incorrigible. You've frightened all the guests into the garden. I apologize, Mother!
Dandini Frightfully sorry, your Majesty.
Queen Not at all. We are definitely amused.
Prince I'll go and fetch them back.
Andromeda I'm coming too!

The Prince and Andromeda exit

Queen I trust you are keeping an eye on my son, Dandini, as I asked you. I want a grandson before I leave this world, and I intend to have one. I have high hopes that Charming will find his bride this very evening.
Dandini Oh rather, your Majesty! I mean, the young fellow's all set on doing his best by you, don't yer know. Trouble is, he's got this bee in his bonnet about marryin' only for love, and all that bally caper.
Queen Ah, just like his father! This grandson will be beautiful, Dandini.
Dandini Indeed, your Majesty.

The Major-Domo enters

Major-Domo The Baron Hardup, and his daughters Snowdrop and Tulip.
Queen How very horticultural!

The Baron and ugly sisters enter

Baron (*bowing*) Your Majesty!
Snowdrop }
Tulip (*together, curtsying*) Your Majesty!
Snowdrop (*to Dandini*) And your Princeship!
Tulip (*likewise*) Your Flagship!

The Queen is surprised, and amused

Queen You have met before I see!
Dandini Er, as a matter of fact, yes, your Majesty.
Queen Present these charming ladies to me.
Snowdrop (*delighted*) Ooooooh!

She digs Tulip in the ribs and, as they are both in full curtsy, sends her sprawling

Dandini This is Miss Snowdrop.

Snowdrop rises

Queen And how old are you, my dear?

Part II, Scene 9

Snowdrop I've just reached twenty-one.
Queen Really. What detained you?
Dandini And this is Miss Tulip.

Tulip rises

Queen I understand you already know this young man.
Tulip Ooooh, yes! We think he's really nobby!
Queen (*rising*) I see. Well, just remember, won't you? (*She smiles*) Boys will be boys!
Tulip (*giggling*) Yes, and girls will be mothers!

Snowdrop gives Tulip another dig in the ribs

Queen I think I'll leave you with your friends—your Flagship!
Dandini Oh no, your Majesty, please!
Queen As you sow, so must you reap! Come, Baron! I want to have a word with the Duchess of Smethwick. Did you know she's just had triplets?
Baron Yes, your Majesty. The Duke was telling me, that only happens once in every two hundred thousand occasions!
Queen So I believe. It baffles me how she ever found time to do the housework!

The Queen exits with the Baron

Snowdrop The first dance is mine, your Princeship! (*She grabs Dandini's arm*)
Tulip No it's not—it's mine! (*She grabs his other arm*)
Snowdrop (*pulling Dandini*) Mine!
Tulip (*likewise*) Mine!
Snowdrop Mine!
Dandini Ladies! Ladies! Please! Remember where you are and all that!
Snowdrop (*to Tulip*) Yes, remember where you are!
Tulip *You* remember!
Snowdrop Now you mustn't misconjugate us, your Princeship. We're very lady-like really.
Tulip Yes, quaite refeened ectually!
Snowdrop Ever so shy. (*Passionately*) Come! Come, O principal Prince of my principality—let's be friendly—let's nestle!
Tulip He's not a tin of condensed milk! (*Coyly*) If you like you can put your arm round some of my waist!
Snowdrop Ignore her funny little ways. She's a bit like the Venus de Milo, you know—beautiful but not all there!
Tulip The cheek! I'd hate to have *your* nerve in *my* tooth! I saw him first and it's my dance! (*She grabs Dandini*)
Snowdrop (*likewise*) Mine!
Tulip Mine!

The ugly sisters squabble. Dandini escapes their clutches

Andromeda enters, carrying a collecting-tin with flags in it. She still has her lollipop. She rattles her tin

Andromeda Hey, Dandy! I'm collecting for charity. Could you donate something for the Old Ladies Home?
Dandini The Old Ladies Home? Certainly! (*Indicating the ugly sisters*) Help yourself!

Dandini exits

The ugly sisters are prevented from following him by Andromeda who holds out her tin under their noses

Andromeda Hey, you! Have you got anything for the Old Ladies Home?
Tulip Please! Not when I'm not eating!
Snowdrop 'Op it, you little horror!

Andromeda howls

Tulip Now you've done it. That's the Prince's baby cousin, that is!
Snowdrop Not the one who shot her parents so she could go to the Orphan's outing?
Tulip That's the one!
Snowdrop Oh lor'! (*Through the din*) 'Ere! All right! Yes! I'll have one! Your Highness! One please! (*Yelling*) Oi!!

Andromeda stops howling

Have you got change of threepence?
Andromeda Hold this!

She gives her lollipop to Snowdrop who takes it by the sticky end. It immediately adheres firmly to her hand. She shakes her hand but can't dislodge it. Eventually she removes it with the other hand, and now it sticks to this one. She appeals to Tulip for help. Tulip removes it, but it sticks to both her hands, and they are glued together. She then removes it with her teeth where it becomes finally jammed. She squeals to Snowdrop in distress. Andromeda finds her change

Snowdrop (*to Tulip*) All right! All right! Hold on! Excuse us, your Highness—er—keep the change!

Snowdrop takes hold of the lollipop-stick and leads off Tulip whose teeth are still clamped to the lollipop

Perhaps we shall find an 'ammer and chisel in the "Ladies"!
Andromeda Hey! My lollipop! Stop thief! Thief!

Andromeda runs off after them

The Queen, Prince and Dandini enter from another entrance, and all the other guests come on

Queen It was very remiss of you to play such a trick on those poor defenceless girls.
Prince Yes, Mother.
Queen It was also very wise! (*She sits*)
Prince Thank you, Mother! And thank *you*, Dandini! (*He sits*)

Part II, Scene 9   51

Queen They do tell me I never forget faces. I shall just have to start trying harder, that's all. Now let us get on with the dancing.

The orchestra gently plays the music for Song No. 14. The guests waltz silently, but the eyes of all the ladies are on the Prince

Prince (*aside*) I look in every face in vain! Though many are fair, and many are beautiful, alas! the bright semblance of the loveliest vision mortal e'er was blessed with meets not my anxious eyes! The hated promise of my betrothal is fast approaching, yet cannot I behold the woman that my heart can incline to! They are all panting for the Prince's crown—they seek not a husband's heart!

Fanfare, off. The music and dancing stop

Major-Domo Her Royal Highness, the Princess "Cenerentola"!

Cinderella appears. She is lightly veiled

The orchestra plays a few bars of the theme. There is a gasp of wonder from the guests

Prince Oh rapture! 'Tis she! Fate has now blessed me! I can know no greater bliss! (*He crosses to meet Cinderella*)
Cinderella (*aside*) 'Tis he! The Prince!
Prince Will not that envious veil, fully removed, permit my eyes to feast upon thy beauty?

Cinderella draws back

Oh disperse that shady cloud, that seems jealous of my happiness. (*He raises her veil*)

There is a further gasp from the guests, and murmurs of "Lovely!" "Where does she come from?" "Beautiful!" etc. The Prince leads her towards the Queen

Prince May I present you to my mother?
Cinderella Your Majesty!
Queen My dear, you are very beautiful.
Prince May I beg you for the first dance, Princess?
Cinderella I should be honoured, your Highness.

Song No. 14

The Prince and Cinderella dance. At a certain moment in the music the Guests join in the dancing. The Prince holds Cinderella in his arms downstage as the Guests circle behind them. The Prince sings. At the end of the dance the Guests withdraw to the sides of the stage

Andromeda runs on

Andromeda Auntie! Auntie! Can we have our pantomime now?
Queen Very well, my dear. Is everything ready?

Andromeda Yes, Auntie. I'll be right back!

Andromeda exits

Music. The Guests arrange themselves as an audience, leaving space in the centre of the stage for the performance and room at the sides for the entrances and exits. The Queen, Prince and Cinderella sit together. The backcloth descends in front of the rostrum across the back completing the stage within a stage

Prince (*during the above*) What pantomime is this, Mother?
Queen A little Harlequinade the child has written. I promised it might be performed before us at the Ball tonight. (*To Cinderella*) Sit here, my dear.
Cinderella Thank you, your Majesty.
Queen Are you enjoying yourself, child?
Cinderella It's ... it's like a dream.

The Prince stares at her

Scene 9a

The Harlequinade

Andromeda enters

Andromeda Ladies and Gentlemen! I entreat
Those who can, please take a seat!
As part of our festive masquerade
We now present—our Harlequinade!

Music: the Overture "Pique Dame" by Franz von Suppé. Andromeda introduces the characters of the Harlequinade as they enter. The Guests applaud politely

The Major-Domo as "Watchman" enters

Here's the Watchman, stern and proper—
Nowadays he's called a copper!

Watchman struts across the stage jauntily swinging his baton

Butcher's rich, with lots of gold,
But has a heart that's mean and cold.

Wormwood as "Butcher" appears at the window of his shop wringing his hands greedily. He bows to Watchman who salutes and continues across the stage and exits

For one thing only does he pine—
The fair and lovely Columbine!

First "crash" in the music

Columbine (Polly Perkins) enters

Part II, Scene 9a

Butcher kneels, clutching his heart, and holding his hands out imploringly. Columbine turns her head away and ignores him

> And her father, Pantaloon,
> Says she must marry Butcher soon!

The Baron, as "Pantaloon", comes out of his house

He turns Columbine to face Butcher. Butcher comes out of the shop and offers her a string of sausages. Columbine refuses them

> Though some may think he's round the bend,
> Old Clown's a true and loyal friend.

Scrubbs enters as "Clown". He spies the boots and goes to grab them

Audience Don't touch!

Clown crosses and joins Pantaloon's group

Andromeda There's only one he thinks should win
Her hand, that's sprightly Harlequin!

Second "crash" in the music

Harlequin springs on

Columbine runs to him. Pantaloon pulls her away and pushes her back towards Butcher again

> But Pantaloon is far from sure,
> For Harlequin is much too poor.

Butcher hands Pantaloon a paper marked "Assets", and gives one end of the string of sausages to Columbine

> Here comes our gentle, comic, hero—
> The droll and melancholy Pierrot.

Buttons, masked, enters as "Pierrot", clutching his breast, and walking solefully, one step at a time. From a pocket in the breast of his smock he extracts a cut-out heart, which he holds delicately in his two hands

Cinderella (*rising*) Why it's——!

The royal party and Guests look at her in surprise

Buttons looks at her, and his "heart" sprouts two little wings (on springs) and flies out of his hands. It glides gently away from him into the wings. He follows, arms outstretched towards his heart, and exits

Andromeda Now see our players on parade
In a gay Harlequinade!

Andromeda exits

Cellos play new "counter-melody" in the music

Harlequin plucks a rose from Pantaloon's window-box and offers it to Columbine. Still holding one end of the sausages she crosses round Pantaloon—who is studying Butcher's "Assets" paper—to Harlequin. Butcher, who still has hold of the other end of the sausages, hauls her back with the sausages and attempts to kiss her, unsuccessfully. This business is repeated. When Columbine sets off for a third time round Pantaloon Clown, who is waiting on the other side of him, takes her end of the sausages from her. Columbine takes the flower from Harlequin and they flirt.

Clown takes the sausages round and round Pantaloon, and then places his end into Pantaloon's hand. Kneeling, Butcher again hauls in the sausages flirtatiously, which spins Pantaloon slowly round like a slow-motion top. Pantaloon looks up from his paper in surprise. On reaching Pantaloon's hand Butcher kisses it, then discovers his mistake. Pantaloon discovers Harlequin and Columbine flirting. He crosses to her, snatches the flower from her, and flings it back at Harlequin.

Third crash in the music

Harlequin gives the flower back to Columbine, from whom Pantaloon snatches it again, hurls it at Harlequin, and marches Columbine into the house. Harlequin shrugs, sticks the flower back into the window-box and exits.

Butcher picks up his "Assets" list, sighs, holds his heart, and goes off into his shop dragging the sausages behind him. Clown steps on the last one, and the whole string slips from Butcher's hand. He exits into the shop. Clown uses the sausages as a skipping rope, and skips round the stage. Butcher discovers his mistake, returns, and chases Clown round the stage wielding a meat cleaver.

Galop

Pantaloon enters. Clown dumps sausages into Pantaloon's hands as he passes him and jumps into Pantaloon's house via the window. Butcher arrives at Pantaloon waving his cleaver, snatches his sausages back, double-takes, realizes who it is, gives the sausages back to Pantaloon with profuse apologies, rushes back to his shop, and returns with a large pie which he presents to Pantaloon, all smiles, and returns to his shop.

Pantaloon goes into his house and returns immediately holding Clown by the ear in one hand, and Pierrot by the ear in the other. Clown carries a small table, and Pierrot a tablecloth. Pantaloon indicates that he expects Butcher for dinner, and that Clown and Pierrot are to lay the table. Pantaloon exits.

Clown, having placed the table in front of the house, takes hold of the other end of Pierrot's tablecloth. It is twisted in the middle. They put it on the table, and then notice the twist in the middle. They turn it over, together, in the same direction. It is still twisted! They turn it back. The same! Still holding each end, they circle round the table to opposite ends. The same! They circle back. Clown lets go of his end, circles round to the back of Pierrot who still holds his end, and turns Pierrot completely over on the spot—thereby untwisting the cloth.

Part II, Scene 9a

Clown puts the pie on the table, looks about to check that they are unobserved, then cuts a wedge out of the pie. Harlequin appears and waves his magic bat, and several birds fly out of the pie (on wires). Harlequin exits. Clown jumps up and down trying to knock the birds down with his knife. Pierrot rushes into the house and returns with a butterfly net. The birds fly off pursued by Clown and Pierrot.

Lady enters with a pram containing a hideous baby, which she parks outside while she enters Butcher's shop. Clown returns anxiously. He peeps into the pie, into Pantaloon's house, and back into the pie again. He spies the Baby in the pram, crosses to it, and takes it out of the pram. It starts to howl. He gives it an enormous baby's bottle from the pram, and crosses towards the pie. Watchman enters, and crosses the stage, stops and studies Clown suspiciously. Clown grins, waves to Watchman, discovers Baby is damp, grins, wipes his hand on his pants, waves to Watchman again, and feeds the Baby. Watchman exits. Clown stuffs the Baby into the pie, and replaces the piece of crust he previously cut out. He takes a large ham hanging in Butcher's window and wraps it in the Baby's shawl, and puts it into the pram with the bottle, and exits.

Lady enters with a chicken from Butcher's shop. Watchman enters and salutes her. She nods and smiles flirtatiously, feeds the bottle to the ham, smiles again at Watchman, double-takes on the ham, and faints. Watchman catches her and carries her off.

Slow passage in the music—flutes and strings

Columbine appears at the window of Pantaloon's house. Harlequin enters. Columbine takes up the flower from Pantaloon's window-box and throws it to him. She steps out of the window and they dance a very short *pas de deux* ending in an embrace UL.

Second half of slow passage

Pierrot's "heart" enters DR, on a wire—followed at a short distance by Pierrot with the butterfly net. He catches his heart. He is about to return it to his breast when he has second thoughts. He steps out of the Harlequinade setting, and presents his heart lovingly to Cinderella, who rises to receive it. He bows to her, steps back into the Harlequinade, and exits dolefully DR.

Final Galop

Clown enters, picks up the sausages, and hangs them over the arms sticking out at the top of the lamppost. He notices how they hang looking like real arms. This gives him an idea for some fun. He fetches the ham the Lady dropped and hangs it on the centre of the lamppost for a body. From Butcher's shop window he adds two salamis as the legs, two turnips for the feet, a pig's head for the face with a black-sausage for the moustache. He adds the tablecloth for a cloak and puts a paper hat on the top. Harlequin turns from Columbine and waves his magic bat at Clown's creation. There is a puff of smoke, the lamppost disappears, and the real Watchman stands in its place. Clown flees in horror pursued by Watchman UL. Harlequin turns back and flirts with Columbine.

Pantaloon comes out of his house with Butcher UR and proceeds to cut open the pie. Lady enters UL and sees them. Butcher pulls the Baby out of the pie. Clown runs in DL and across the stage pursued by Watchman. Clown exits DR. Lady screams and points at Butcher. Watchman stops, then chases Butcher, who still carries the Baby, round the stage and off DR, followed by Lady. Pantaloon spies Harlequin kissing Columbine and chases after them. They exit UL. Pierrot enters UR, spies Harlequin, Columbine and Pantaloon running in DL, assumes they're after him and runs off DR, followed by Harlequin, Columbine, and Pantaloon. Butcher, chased by Watchman and Lady runs on UR. Butcher is in time to see Pantaloon running off DR, and chases after him still followed by Watchman and Lady.

Pierrot, Harlequin, Columbine, Pantaloon, Butcher, Clown (now armed with his red-hot poker which he applies eagerly to Butcher's bottom), Watchman, and Lady enter in single running line UR, and do a marking-time chase across the stage. This turns into a circle (i.e. Pierrot following Lady) with everyone chasing everyone. Butcher passes the Baby to Pantaloon, who passes it to Columbine, who passes it to Harlequin, who passes it to Pierrot. Lady looks over her shoulder and sees that Pierrot now has her Baby. She turns round, as do all the other characters, and the chase continues in the opposite direction, until they all collapse in a heap around Harlequin triumphant holding his bat victoriously over his head, whilst Columbine hangs lovingly about his neck

End of the Harlequinade

The royal group and Guests applaud

The performers take their bows and exit. The Guests exit

The backcloth rises

Queen (*rising*) Delightful. Did you enjoy it, my dear!
Cinderella Very much, your Majesty.
Queen I'm so glad. Now, if you'll excuse me ...

Cinderella curtsies

The Queen exits

Prince (*drawing Dandini to one side*) Who *is* she, Dandini? Where does she come from?
Dandini Haven't a notion, your Highness. I'll make enquiries.

Dandini exits

Prince (*approaching Cinderella*) Your Highness, please tell me, have we never met before?
Cinderella Your Highness, I ... I feel sure it ... and yet ...
Prince Strangely ... ? Not knowing for sure ... ? As in another dream?
Cinderella Somewhere far ...
Prince   Midst trees ...
Cinderella   And birds ...

Part II, Scene 9a

Prince And flowers!
That's it. It was amidst flowers! On a Summer's day!

Song No. 15

The Prince sings and Cinderella joins him

As the song finishes the clock begins to strike midnight. The music stops. Cinderella looks with horror at the clock

Cinderella The clock! Ah me, the dread midhour of night!
Oh woe is me!
Prince Sweet Princess, why this plight?
Cinderella Forget "The Princess". She no longer lives.
To you, her heart, poor Cinderella gives—
Farewell!

Cinderella runs off downstage

Prince But what ails thee? What is it? Quick, Dandini, we must follow her. Princess! Princess!

Dandini and the Prince run off after Cinderella

Dandini (*as they go*) Princess!

The Queen and her Guests begin to surge on, wondering at the commotion. Behind them, on the twelfth clock chime, the figure of Cinderella (her stand-in)—in her rags once again—is seen to enter on the rostrum upstage and run across it

The Guests are frozen in magic stillness as:

Aconite appears on the rostrum and bars Cinderella's way

Aconite At last! This is my great triumphant hour!
This is the crowning glory of my power!
Now all shall fear me—I shall hold full sway,
And soon infest the country night and day!

Aconite disappears. Cinderella runs off—now seen by only the Queen

The Guests are animated again

Dandini (*off*) This way, your Highness! She came this way!

Dandini and the Prince enter upstage on the rostrum

Prince (*moving downstage*) Mother! Did you see her?
Queen My son, I wonder if we should interfere in this. There was an aura of magic about that child. Perhaps this is the way she wishes it to be.
Prince No, Mother. I must find her. (*To the Guests*) Why are you standing there? Look for her!

The Guests exit in confusion

Dandini comes down to the Prince from the rostrum with Cinderella's slipper

(*To Dandini*) Is there no sign of her?

The Major-Domo enters

Dandini Your Highness, I found this on the stairway. The Princess must have dropped it as she ran off, don't yer know!
Queen How dainty it is!
Prince Dandini! Order my soldiers and courtiers to search the land until they find the maiden whose foot shall fit this shoe. Do it at once!
Dandini Your Highness. (*He bows*)

Dandini exits

Prince Major-Domo, issue this decree. By Royal Command—every maiden in the land shall try on this shoe. Whomsoever it may fit shall be brought to the palace, and treated with all royal honours. If she consents, she shall be my Princess!
Queen My son!
Prince Do it, Major-Domo!
Major-Domo Your Highness! (*He bows*)

The Major-Domo exits

Prince It is my last hope, Mother.
Queen My blessing on you, my dear son. I hope you may find what you are seeking.

The Queen exits

Left alone, the Prince sings a short reprise of Song 14, slowly and quietly

The Prince exits at the end of the reprise

The Baron—tipsy—enters, supported by Polly Perkins and Princess Andromeda

Andromeda I do think it's all most frightfully sad. Poor old Charmers!
Baron I don't think you should have any more to drink, your Royal Highness, your face is beginning to get blurred. Great Scott! What are my boots doing there! Must remember to take 'em home! (*He staggers towards the boots*)
Audience Don't touch!
Baron Quite right! Quite right! Quite forgot! But it's true what you said ... Life's very sad. Did you ever know my wife, little girl?
Polly No, Baron.
Baron For twenty years my wife and I were ecstatically happy.
Polly Then what happened?
Baron We met! When I think of her, my grief is so sincere that I cry, cry, my gal, cry ink! (*He sobs*)
Andromeda Here! You're not supposed to come to a Ball to bawl your eyes out! Cease! Desist, little blubbering Baron! Chuck it!
Baron That's exactly what my wife did! The path of my true love has always

been full of bumps. The first girl I loved liked me but her *father* didn't! And the second girl's *father* liked me, but *she* didn't! And the third girl— she liked me and her father liked me ...

Andromeda
Polly } (*together*) So what happened?

Baron Her husband didn't! (*He sits*) But my saddest story of all is yet to come. Would you like to hear it?

Andromeda
Polly } (*together*) Please do tell us! (*They sit on his knees and sing*)

Song No. 16 After The Ball
by Charles K. Harris and A. St. John

Andromeda **Polly**	Two sweet little gentle maidens Sit on an old man's knees And beg him to tell them a story— And one that is true if you please! Did you not marry for love then? Would *you* rather live alone?
Andromeda	Don't you like children, Baron? Had you *no* happy home?
Baron	Oh, I had a sweetheart years, years ago ... Where she is now, girls, you soon will know. Listen to the story, I will tell you all— I believed her faithless after the Ball—

After the Ball is over,
After the break of morn,
After the dancers leaving,
After the stars are gone;
Many a heart is aching,
If you could read them all;
Many the hopes that have vanished,
After the Ball ...

Brightly the lights were flashing
Within the grand ballroom,
Softly the charming music
Played the old sweet tunes,
Softly there came my sweetheart
And whispered in love's sweet tone—
"Fetch me a glass of water
And I will wait alone".
When I returned, dears, after,
Beside her stood a man
Kissing my own heart's darling
As only lovers can!
Down fell the glass all broken,

>   Broken beyond recall,
>   Like my fond hopes 'twas shattered
>   After the Ball ...

The Stage Manager enters with words for the audience. The Queen, Dandini, Major-Domo, and Guests enter and join in the chorus

All
>   After the Ball is over,
>   After the break of morn,
>   After the dancers leaving,
>   After the stars are gone;
>   Many a heart is aching
>   If you could read them all;
>   Many the hopes that have vanished,
>   After the Ball ...

Baron
>   Long years have passed since then, girls,
>   Other wives I have wed,
>   Rememb'ring my heart's own lost love,
>   True to her though she's dead!
>   Oh, how she tried to tell me,
>   Oh, how she would explain,
>   Raging was I and mad-den'd
>   And her pleadings were in vain.
>   One day, a long lost letter
>   Came from that stranger man,
>   He was her elder brother—
>   That's how the letter ran.
>   That, dears, is why I'm lonely,
>   Have no real home at all,
>   I broke my darling's heart dear,
>   After the Ball (*He sobs*)

The Guests dance as they sing

All
>   After the Ball is over,
>   After the break of morn,
>   After the dancers leaving,
>   After the stars are gone;
>   Many a heart is aching,
>   If you could read them all;
>   Many the hopes that have vanished,
>   After the Ball ...

As they repeat the chorus very quietly, the Lights fade

A single spot lights the lonely figure of Prince Charming as he walks sadly across the rostrum at the back of the ballroom

>   After the Ball is over, *etc., etc.*

Scene 10

A room in Hardup Hall (frontcloth)
The furniture painted on the cloth includes two canaries in a golden cage
Buttons enters with a chair which he places C
Buttons Howdy, kids!
Audience Howdy, Buttons!

The wailing and groaning of the ugly sisters is heard, off

Tulip and Snowdrop enter, pushing a wheelbarrow in which lies the prostrate, unconscious and inebriated Baron

Snowdrop Oooooh! Oooooh!
Tulip Ooohoooooo!
Snowdrop It's not fair! It's not fair!
Tulip They should be punished. (*There is a strange whistling in her speech*)
Buttons What's the matter, Snowdrop?
Snowdrop We've been tricked!
Tulip Deceived!
Snowdrop We've been looked over and overlooked!
Tulip A couple of "yes" girls who never had a chance to talk!
Snowdrop We thought we were dancing with the Prince, and it wasn't the Prince at all!
Buttons Who was it?
Snowdrop ⎫
Tulip ⎭ (*together*) His valet! (*They both howl again*)
Buttons Well, I tried to warn you!
Snowdrop Oh, I must sit down, me feet are killing me! (*She flops into the chair*)
Tulip And I've lost me teeth! (*She bares her teeth and we see a big black gap where her front teeth used to be*)
Buttons Where are they?
Tulip In the Princess's lollipop.
Buttons What were you doing with the Princess's lollipop?
Snowdrop We got stuck with it! Oooh, me feet! (*She throws off her shoes*) Me feet! I just can't get into a seventeen-and-a-half shoe anymore. Where are me slippers?
Tulip (*spying the boots and approaching them*) Are these them?
Audience Don't touch!
Buttons So you're not marrying the Prince after all?
Snowdrop You shut up!
Tulip Anyway, I don't intend to be married until I'm thirty!
Snowdrop You mean you don't intend to be thirty until you're married!
Baron (*coming to, singing*) "When you are in love, it's the loveliest night of the year!"
Tulip Papa's waking up!
Snowdrop Must be opening time!

Baron Watcha, gals! Or should I say Princesses?

Snowdrop and Tulip howl

(*Surprised*) You know I never would have believed it, but drinking suits you gals. It makes you look quite beautiful! Quite beautiful!

Snowdrop ⎫
Tulip ⎭ (*together*) But we haven't been drinking!

Baron I know. But I have!

Snowdrop and Tulip howl again

Never mind, gals, don't be discouraged. In this world there's a man for every girl, and a girl for every man. You can't improve on an arrangement like that!

Tulip We don't want to improve on it. We just want to get in on it!
Baron Hold on there, Tulip. What's happened to your two front——
Tulip Oh, be quiet! I don't want to talk about it.
Baron Talk about the Cumberland Gap! What happened?
Tulip It's very embarrassing! (*She sings*)

Song No. 17

Baron I like that! Let's all sing it! Let's have a sing-song!
Snowdrop What a good idea, Papa. Come on, bring on the Hymn Sheet, and we'll get all the boys and girls to sing.

The Stage Manager enters with the words

Tulip, Snowdrop and the Baron do the house number in the usual way (dividing the house, etc.)

When the house number is finished the Stage Manager removes the words

There is a fanfare, off

The Major-Domo enters and reads from a scroll

Major-Domo Oh yes! Oh yes! Oh yes!
"Whereas it happened last night at the Ball
A maiden let a crystal slipper fall,
The Prince has vowed, and bidden me declare it,
He'll marry any lady who can wear it!"
Snowdrop Well I say! Did you cop an earful of that?
Tulip We might become Princesses after all!
Snowdrop Perhaps Queen one day! Oooh, undo a button somewhere and let me shriek!
Tulip And all I have to do is to get me foot into that crystal slipper!
Snowdrop You couldn't get that foot into the Crystal Palace!
Major-Domo Bring in the slipper!

Dandini enters with the slipper

Tulip Ooooh, look! It's him!!

Part II, Scene 10

Snowdrop Let me get at him! Let me get at him!

Buttons and the Baron restrain the ugly sisters

Tulip Call the Fire Brigade!
Buttons Why the Fire Brigade?
Tulip To put him out!
Baron Girls, remember, this may be your last chance!
Snowdrop Yes, right! Well I'll just wait until I'm Queen, then I'll chuck him in a dungeon!
Major-Domo Who will be the first to try on the shoe?
Snowdrop Me!
Tulip Me!

They both rush to sit down on the chair. Their bottoms collide and they land on the floor, either side of the chair. The Baron helps Tulip up. The Major-Domo helps Snowdrop up, and puts her into the chair

Major-Domo Now, try on the shoe.

There is a roll of drums. Dandini tries the shoe on Snowdrop

Dandini It doesn't fit!
Snowdrop Here, you're not trying properly. (*She snatches the shoe from him and tussles with it, but it still perches on the end of her foot*) Wretched thing! It must have shrunk! (*She rises, trying to jam the shoe on*)
Tulip What do you expect with a pair of kippers like that?
Snowdrop Now I can't get it off!

The others all join in a tug of war to get the shoe off Snowdrop. Meanwhile Tulip sneaks round behind them and sits. They finally wrench the shoe off Snowdrop's foot

Tulip My turn! My turn!

Another roll of drums as Dandini tries the shoe on Tulip's foot. It fits

Dandini It fits!!
All It fits!!!
Baron If there's a drop of brandy, I'll faint. If there isn't I won't bother!
Major-Domo It's a fit!
Dandini More like a bally paralytic stroke!
Snowdrop Just a minute! Just a minute! There's something supercilious going on here. (*She crosses to Tulip and gives her leg a sharp tug—it comes away in her hand, being an artificial leg*) Oooh, you little cheat!
Tulip Spoilsport!
Baron That's very naughty!
Snowdrop How dare you!
Tulip If we was in India *you*'d be sacred!

Dandini retrieves the shoe

Major-Domo If there's nobody else we must move on.
Buttons Hey! Wait a moment! What 'bout Miss Cindy?

Dandini Have you another daughter, Baron?
Snowdrop⎫
Tulip   ⎭ (*together*) No he hasn't!
Baron Yes I have!
Buttons Good for you, Baron.
Snowdrop But that shoe won't fit her! She's known all over as Bargey Margey!
Buttons That's not true!
Tulip Got the biggest beetle-crushers in the county!
Baron Fetch her, Buttons!
Buttons Yes, sir!!!

Buttons exits

Tulip You're wasting your time!
Dandini Is your wife at home, Baron?
Baron My wife is in Heaven, dear boy.
Dandini Oh I *am* sorry—I mean I'm glad, of course—er—I mean—I'm surprised!

Cinderella enters

Cinderella You sent for me, Papa?
Baron Yes, my child. This gentleman wants you to try on this shoe. The Prince has sent him.
Cinderella The Prince . . . ? I don't think I ought to.
Major-Domo It is a Royal Command.
Cinderella Very well.

Cinderella sits. There is a roll of drums as Dandini tries the shoe on Cinderella

Dandini It fits!
Major-Domo   At Last!
Baron   My child!
Buttons   Yippeeeeeeee!
Snowdrop Oooh! You could knock me down with a feather!

Tulip produces a feather and swipes Snowdrop over the head with it. Snowdrop collapses at the Baron's feet

Dandini (*bowing to Cinderella*) You are requested to accompany us to the palace.

Cinderella rises

Snowdrop (*crossing to exit*) Well! I have never been so insulted!
Buttons Yes, they soon had you taped!
Tulip (*likewise*) It's a diabolitical liberty!
Snowdrop Anyway, it's their loss! *I* don't care, do you?
Tulip Not a bit!
Snowdrop⎫
Tulip   ⎭ (*together*) We don't care!

Part II, Scene 11

Tulip and Snowdrop burst into tears and exit

Baron Come, Cinderella, we must go to the palace.
Major-Domo I will see that her carriage is prepared.

The Major-Domo exits

Dandini Are you ready, Cinderella?
Cinderella Yes. But may I speak to Buttons first?
Dandini Of course. Will you come with us, Baron?
Baron Most kind! Most kind!

Dandini and the Baron exit

Buttons So the Princess at the Ball was you all the time!
Cinderella And you knew all the time, didn't you, Buttons?
Buttons Uhuh!
Cinderella You were there too, weren't you?
Buttons Uhuh!
Cinderella Buttons, this won't make any difference to us, will it? You'll come and live with us at the palace, won't you?
Buttons Oh, I wouldn't want to do that, Miss Cindy.
Cinderella There'll always be a place for you in my heart.
Buttons I know that, Miss Cindy, and I'll come to the wedding and everything—but as for living at the palace with you and the Prince—well—it's like that story I used to tell you about the little old sparrow and the canaries. Do you remember? (*He gazes up at the bird-cage on the backcloth*)
Cinderella Yes, Buttons, but ...
Buttons Remember?

Buttons and Cinderella sing holding hands

Song No. 18

At the appropriate moment the Stage Manager enters with the words for the audience and everyone sings

At the end of the song Cinderella and Buttons release each other's hands and exit in opposite directions

SCENE 11

The royal palace—Cinderella's wedding (fullstage)

There is a gauze backcloth upstage which will be lit later to reveal the fairy coach and horses

Queen Mariana, the Baron (in a frockcoat and smoking a cigar), Andromeda, Buttons and Dandini, who is holding hands with Polly Perkins, are posed formally in a family group C as for a wedding photograph. Wormwood is operating an old camera, while Scrubbs holds the flash pan

When the frontcloth from the previous scene is raised there is a flash, and the broker's men exit with their paraphernalia

The wedding group sing

Song No. 19

At the end of the song everyone exits

Walk down of cast

Buttons collects the boots and thanks the audience for looking after them

The Prince and Cinderella are the last to walk down and they sing a short reprise together

Song No. 3 (reprise)

Prince (*speaking*) 'Twas like a dream, I think we do but dream,
   Yet if it's true, 'tis better than to seem.
   Though all we've gained is more than is our due,
   Yet more we need—(*to the audience*)—we need your favours too!
Cinderella We creatures are but spirits framed of air,
   And though made light of, as you were aware,
   Yet still our power is greater than it seems
   If we bring happy thoughts and pleasant dreams.
   If love is happiness—and laughter too,
   May you be blessed with both, my friends—adieu!

The Lights fade up behind the gauze backcloth and the fairy coach and horses appear. The gauze rises and the Prince and Cinderella walk upstage and climb into the coach

   The Stage Manager enters with the words for the audience

Everyone sings

Song No. 16 (reprise)

All   After the Ball is over,
   After the break of morn,
   After the dancers leaving,
   After the stars are gone;
   Many a heart is aching,
   If you could read them all;
   Many the hopes that have vanished
   After the Ball . . .

CURTAIN

FURNITURE AND PROPERTY LIST

PART I

SCENE 1

On stage: Nil

Personal: **Fairy Flora:** wand (used throughout)

SCENE 2

On stage: Sticks of firewood

Off stage: Words of Song No. 2 chorus on easel **(Stage Manager)**
Words of Song No. 4 chorus on easel **(Stage Manager)**
Small bundle of firewood **(Cinderella)**

Personal: **Dandini:** monocle (used throughout), hat
Prince: hunting horn, hat
Cinderella: basket of daisies

SCENE 3

On stage: Nil

SCENE 4

On stage: Nil

Off stage: Words of "Beer, Beer, Glorious Beer" chorus on easel **(Stage Manager)**
Words of Song No. 6 chorus on easel **(Stage Manager)**
Pair of brightly coloured boots **(Buttons)**
Wooden bucket with a hole **(Scrubbs)**
Straw **(Scrubbs)**
Knife **(Scrubbs)**
Stone **(Scrubbs)**

Personal: **Baron:** letter, large spotted handkerchief, kipper under hat
Wormwood: notebook, pencil, cards
Scrubbs: bowler hat with two small protruding horns

SCENE 5

On stage: 2 windows (practical)
Large fireplace. *On mantelpiece:* 2 large candlesticks, clock

Chair. *By it:* bowl of potatoes and knife (for **Cinderella**)
Large basket skip
Kitchen table. *On it:* large red chequered tablecloth, empty rum bottle
Chair
Chest
Cupboard. *In it:* fan, joint of meat parcelled up, potty
Old "Victorian" trick telephone on the wall
Large pair of colourful ladies' drawers full of holes
Vase containing a flower
Pair of brightly coloured boots downstage (NB. These remain downstage for the duration of the performance)
Bucket and cloth upstage

Personal: **Cinderella:** piece of bread in apron pocket
Dandini: 3 invitation cards
Wormwood: notebook, pencil, form
Scrubbs: notebook, pencil

SCENE 6

On stage: Nil

Off stage: 2 chairs **(Buttons)**
Small handcart with notice on the side as in text. *In it:* spade, large cloth, 2 caps and covers, 2 bowls of liquid mud, 2 towels, powder and large powder puff, make-up tray containing lip-rouge, brushes, eye shadow, eyebrow pencil and mascara, enormous pair of pincers, taper, matches, jar of gravy **(Scrubbs)**
Snowdrop's wig **(Buttons)**
Corsets **(Buttons)**
Words of Song No. 10 chorus on easel **(Stage Manager)**
Snowdrop's "Little Bo-Peep" costume **(Cinderella)**

Personal: **Wormwood:** cigarette holder, comb in pocket

SCENE 7

On stage: 2 windows
Large fireplace. *On mantelpiece:* 2 large candlesticks, clock
3 chairs
Large basket skip
Kitchen table. *By it:* cabbage wrapped up like a bouquet
Chest
Cupboard

Off stage: Words of Song No. 11 chorus on easel **(Stage Manager)**
Pumpkin, rat, lizards, mice **(Fairies)**
Large, sparkling invitation card **(Fairy)**

During Black-out on page 37

Strike: Fireplace, pumpkin, rat, lizards, mice

Set: Fairy coach and horses

Cinderella

Personal: **Baron:** invitation card
Buttons: bags of sweets, piece of paper

PART II

SCENE 8

On stage: Victorian vintage automobile with one wheel removed and placed to one side. *In car:* spray-gun. *Under bonnet:* giant moth on wires. *At front:* starting handle
Spanner
Pump

Personal: **Snowdrop:** rose
Scrubbs: envelope with stamps
Major-Domo: cigarettes
Bear: box of matches

SCENE 9

On stage: Large ornate clock
Low rostrum with steps and pillars. *On it:* 2 chairs
Chairs

Off stage: Collecting tin with flags **(Andromeda)**

Personal: **Major-Domo:** staff
Andromeda: huge lollipop, coins
Snowdrop: coins

SCENE 9a

On stage: Butcher's shop cut-out. *Hanging in window:* large ham, 2 salamis, 2 turnips, pig's head, black sausage
Pierrot's house cut-out
Lamppost

Off stage: String of sausages, paper marked "ASSETS" **(Butcher)**
Meat cleaver **(Butcher)**
Large pie containing birds on wires **(Butcher)**
Small table **(Clown)**
Tablecloth **(Pierrot)**
Butterfly net **(Pierrot)**
Pram containing hideous baby and enormous baby bottle **(Lady)**
Chicken **(Lady)**
Red hot poker **(Clown)**
Words of "After The Ball" chorus on easel **(Stage Manager)**

Personal: **Watchman:** baton
Pierrot: cut-out heart with wings in pocket
Clown: knife, paper hat in pocket
Harlequin: magic bat

At the end of the Harlequinade on page 56

Strike: Butcher's shop cut-out
Pierrot's house cut-out
All Harlequinade properties

Scene 10

On stage: Nil

Off stage: Chair *(Buttons)*
Wheelbarrow **(Tulip** and **Snowdrop)**
Words of Song No. 17 on easel **(Stage Manager)**
Scroll **(Major-Domo)**
Cinderella's slipper **(Dandini)**
Words of Song No. 18 chorus on easel **(Stage Manager)**

Personal: **Tulip:** artificial leg, large feather

Scene 11

On stage: Old camera (for **Wormwood**)
Flash pan (for **Scrubbs**)
Fairy coach and horses behind gauze backcloth

Personal: **Baron:** cigar

LIGHTING PLOT

Property fittings required: nil

Various interior and exterior settings

PART I, SCENE 1

To open: Moonlight downstage

Cue 1	**Aconite:** "In phantom revels join—beware!" *Fade moonlight slowly, bringing up cold dawn effect downstage*	(Page 2)
Cue 2	**Fairies** (singing): "Hail the light!" *Snow effect*	(Page 2)
Cue 3	The **Fairies** cower and shiver DR, covering up their heads *Bring up lighting on Snow Queen*	(Page 2)

PART I, SCENE 2

To open: **Snow Queen** lit with snow effect, winter daylight effect downstage

Cue 4	The **Fairies** exit *Increase lighting slightly overall, cut snow effect*	(Page 3)
Cue 5	**Fairy Flora** raises her wand *Fade up on* **Cinderella**	(Page 5)
Cue 6	**Fairy Flora** raises her wand *Black-out on* **Cinderella**	(Page 5)
Cue 7	**Cinderella:** "No, at all seasons!" *Slow fade up on* **Snow Queen**	(Page 9)
Cue 8	**Cinderella:** "... becomes a sparkling diamond!" *Slow fade up to overall sunshine effect*	(Page 9)

PART I, SCENE 3

To open: Continue fade up from previous scene

No cues

PART I, SCENE 4

To open: General exterior lighting downstage

No cues

PART I, SCENE 5

To open: General interior lighting

Cue 9   At the end of Song No. 9   (Page 28)
            Black-out

PART I, SCENE 6

To open: General interior lighting

No cues

PART I, SCENE 7

To open: General interior lighting

Cue 10   **Aconite** exits   (Page 37)
            Fade to spot on **Fairy Flora**

Cue 11   **Flora:** "For Cinderella's glorious hour!"   (Page 37)
            Fade up to previous lighting

Cue 12   **Flora:** "Fairy horses! Fairy coach!"   (Page 37)
            Black-out. When ready snap on full overall lighting

PART II, SCENE 8

To open: General daylight effect downstage

No cues

PART II, SCENE 9

To open: Crossfade from previous scene to overall interior lighting

No cues

PART II, SCENE 9a

To open: As previous scene with lighting concentrated slightly c

Cue 13   The royal group and Guests applaud   (Page 56)
            Overall interior lighting

Cue 14   As everyone sings the final chorus of "After The Ball"   (Page 60)
            Start slow fade with follow spot on **Prince Charming** *upstage*

PART II, SCENE 10

To open: General interior lighting

No cues

PART II, SCENE 11

To open: General interior lighting on wedding group

Cue 15   **Cinderella:** "... my friends—adieu!"   (Page 66)
            Fade up on fairy coach and horses

EFFECTS PLOT

PART I

Cue 1	**Fairies:** "Hail the light!" *Wind*	(Page 2)
Cue 2	To open SCENE 2 *Low moan of icy wind, continue throughout scene*	(Page 2)
Cue 3	**Flora:** "... sweet sunshine to the earth once more!" *Hunting horns in distance, sounds of the chase*	(Page 3)
Cue 4	**Flora:** "... whom your Queen befriends." *Hunting horns nearer*	(Page 3)
Cue 5	Everyone exits after Song No. 2 *Hunting horn*	(Page 4)
Cue 6	**Flora:** "... living in thy heart!" *Hunting horn approaching*	(Page 5)
Cue 7	**Dandini:** "I think I hear them coming." *Fast galloping horse, followed by loud crash, neighs and yells*	(Page 6)
Cue 8	**Baron:** "... I'm ten payments behind on now!" *Loud doorknock* L	(Page 20)
Cue 9	**Snowdrop:** "I had to pay for it!" *Telephone*	(Page 21)
Cue 10	**Snowdrop:** "Never heard of chamber music?" *Loud doorknock* L	(Page 21)
Cue 11	The **Baron** places the vase on the skip *Loud doorknock* L	(Page 21)
Cue 12	Everyone squeezes under the table *Doorknock* L	(Page 21)
Cue 13	**Scrubbs** (*shouting off*): "Effects!!" *In rapid succession: loud burst of wind, galloping horse, gunshots, motor horns, steam trains, woman screaming*	(Page 22)
Cue 14	**Scrubbs:** "One cloth, table." *Telephone inside skip*	(Page 22)
Cue 15	**Scrubbs:** "Overtime!" *Telephone inside cupboard*	(Page 24)
Cue 16	**Wormwood:** "One new-fangled telephone!" *Telephone*	(Page 24)
Cue 17	**Scrubbs:** "I'm all right now." *Telephone inside chest*	(Page 25)

Cue 18	**Wormwood** closes the cupboard door and double-takes *Telephone inside cupboard*	(Page 26)
Cue 19	**Wormwood** crosses to the skip and sighs. The others sigh too *Telephone inside skip*	(Page 26)
Cue 20	**Snowdrop:** "I'm going as Little Bo-Peep!" *Doorbell*	(Page 29)
Cue 21	**Flora:** "Fairy horses! Fairy coach!" *Flash*	(Page 37)

PART II

Cue 22	To open SCENE 8 *Vintage car approaching and then receding as in text*	(Page 40)
Cue 23	**Tulip:** "Here comes another one!" *Sound of vintage car passing*	(Page 41)
Cue 24	**Snowdrop** turns herself into a picture of seductiveness *Vintage car approaching, passing, then tremendous crash*	(Page 41)
Cue 25	The **Bear** lets the tyre down *Loud hiss of escaping air*	(Page 42)
Cue 26	The **Bear** lets down the tyre *Loud hiss of escaping air*	(Page 42)
Cue 27	The **Bear** turns the starting handle *Engine starts*	(Page 42)
Cue 28	**Snowdrop** pulls out the choke *Loud explosion, cut engine*	(Page 43)
Cue 29	The **Baron** turns the starting handle *Engine starts*	(Page 43)
Cue 30	**Baron:** "And away we go!" *Loud explosion, cut engine*	(Page 43)
Cue 31	**Major-Domo:** "... and His Royal Highness, Prince Charming!" *Fanfare*	(Page 47)
Cue 32	**Prince:** "... had let her out!" *Fanfare*	(Page 47)
Cue 33	**Prince:** "... they seek not a husband's heart!" *Fanfare*	(Page 51)
Cue 34	**Harlequin** waves his magic bat at **Clown**'s creation *Puff of smoke*	(Page 55)
Cue 35	As Song No. 15 finishes *Clock strikes midnight*	(Page 57)
Cue 36	When Song No. 17 is finished *Fanfare*	(Page 62)
Cue 37	To open SCENE 11 *Flash from flash pan*	(Page 65)

MADE AND PRINTED IN GREAT BRITAIN BY
LATIMER TREND & COMPANY LTD PLYMOUTH
MADE IN ENGLAND